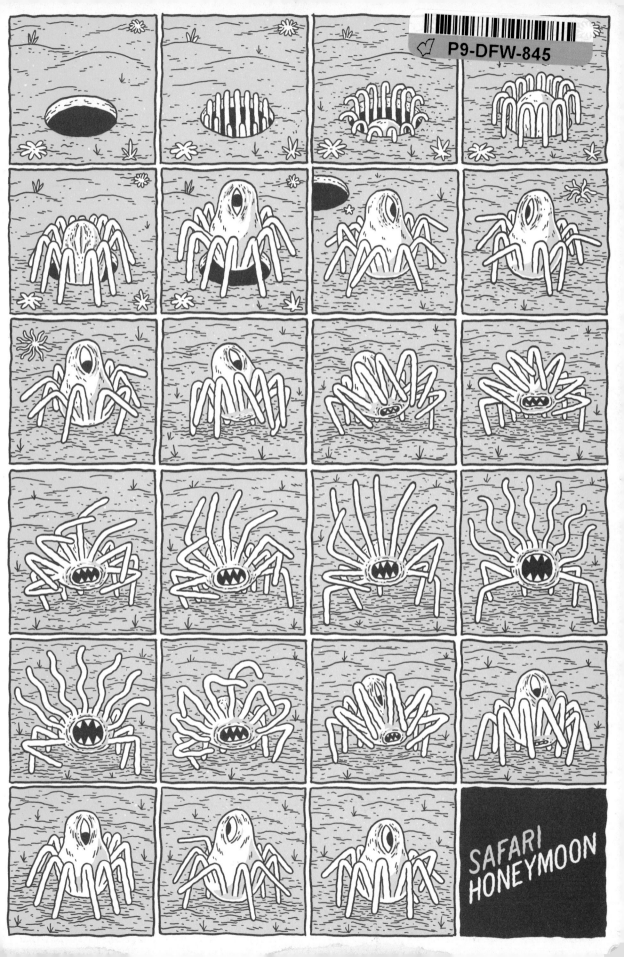

SAFARI
HONEYMOON

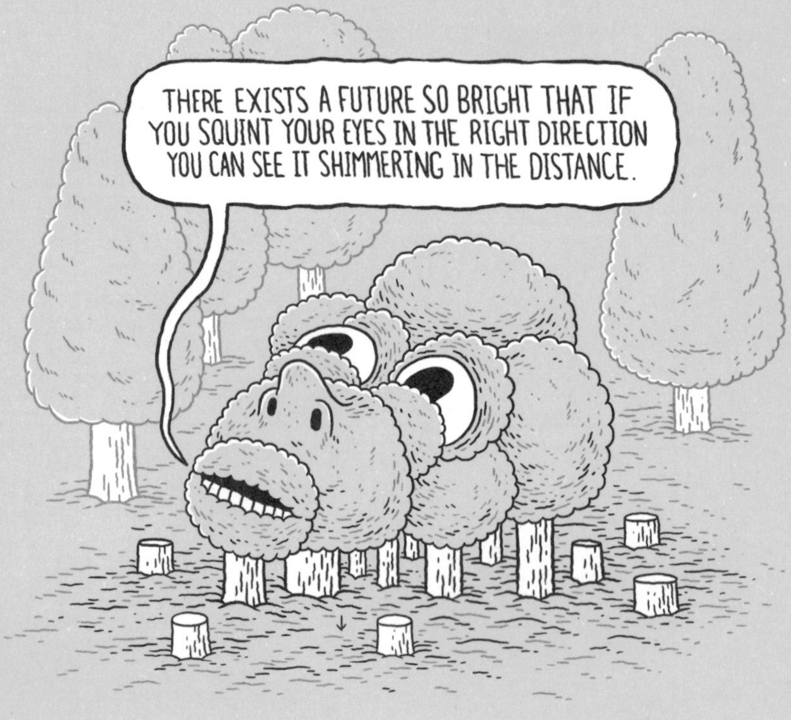
THERE EXISTS A FUTURE SO BRIGHT THAT IF YOU SQUINT YOUR EYES IN THE RIGHT DIRECTION YOU CAN SEE IT SHIMMERING IN THE DISTANCE.

PUBLISHED BY KOYAMA PRESS KOYAMAPRESS.COM
FIRST EDITION: MAY 2014 ISBN: 978-1-927668-04-7 PRINTED IN CHINA THE AUTHOR WOULD LIKE TO ACKNOWLEDGE THE ONTARIO ARTS COUNCIL FOR THEIR FINANCIAL SUPPORT IN THE DEVELOPMENT OF THIS BOOK. KOYAMA PRESS GRATEFULLY ACKNOWLEDGES THE CANADA COUNCIL FOR THE ARTS FOR THEIR SUPPORT OF OUR PUBLISHING PROGRAM.
MUCH LOVE AND GRATITUDE TO JINETTE FOR HER KINDNESS AND HER DELICIOUSLY INSPIRATIONAL COOKING.
THANKS ALWAYS TO THE AMAZING ANNIE KOYAMA!

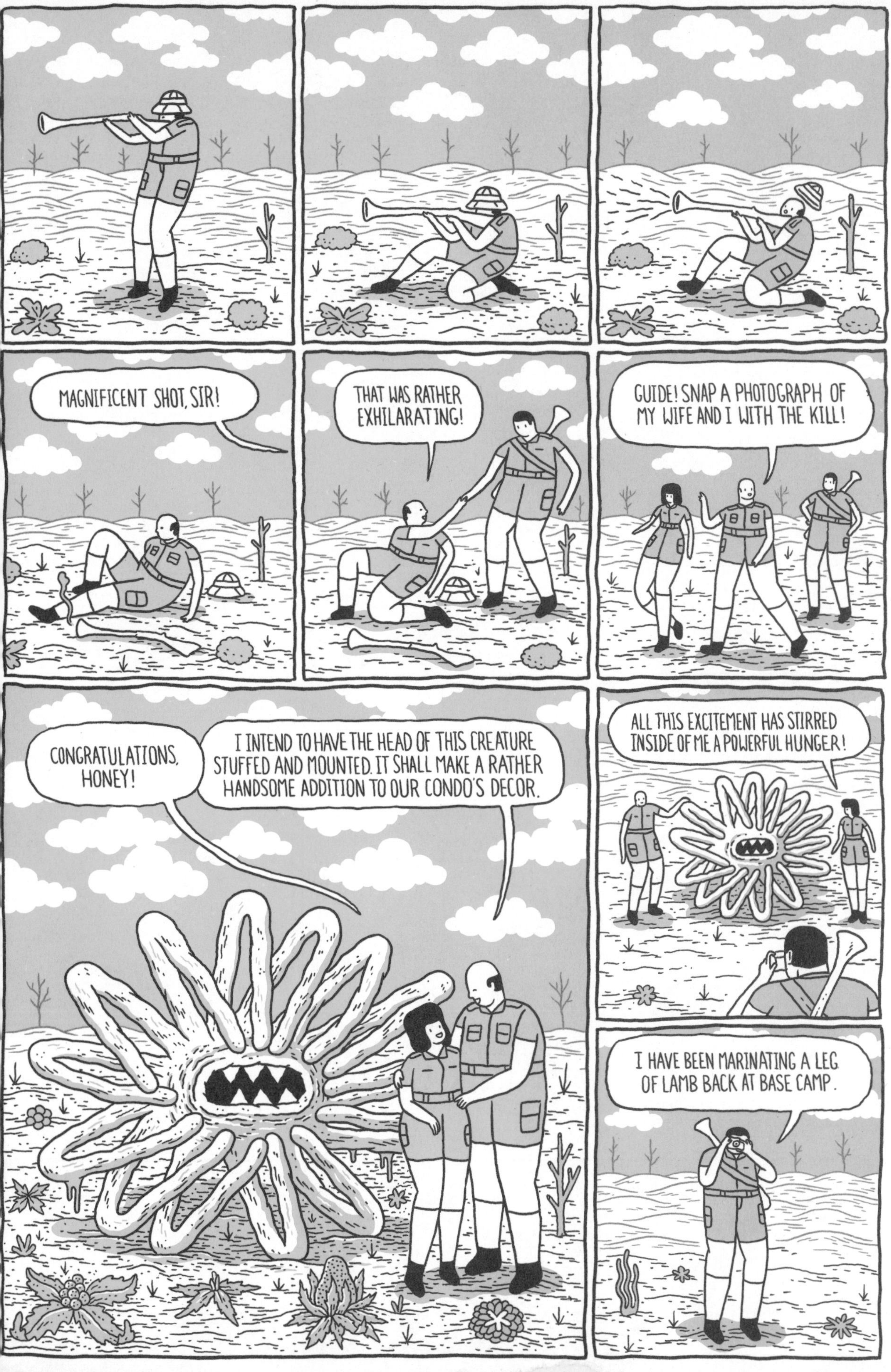
MAGNIFICENT SHOT, SIR!
THAT WAS RATHER EXHILARATING!
GUIDE! SNAP A PHOTOGRAPH OF MY WIFE AND I WITH THE KILL!
CONGRATULATIONS, HONEY!
I INTEND TO HAVE THE HEAD OF THIS CREATURE STUFFED AND MOUNTED. IT SHALL MAKE A RATHER HANDSOME ADDITION TO OUR CONDO'S DECOR.
ALL THIS EXCITEMENT HAS STIRRED INSIDE OF ME A POWERFUL HUNGER!
I HAVE BEEN MARINATING A LEG OF LAMB BACK AT BASE CAMP.

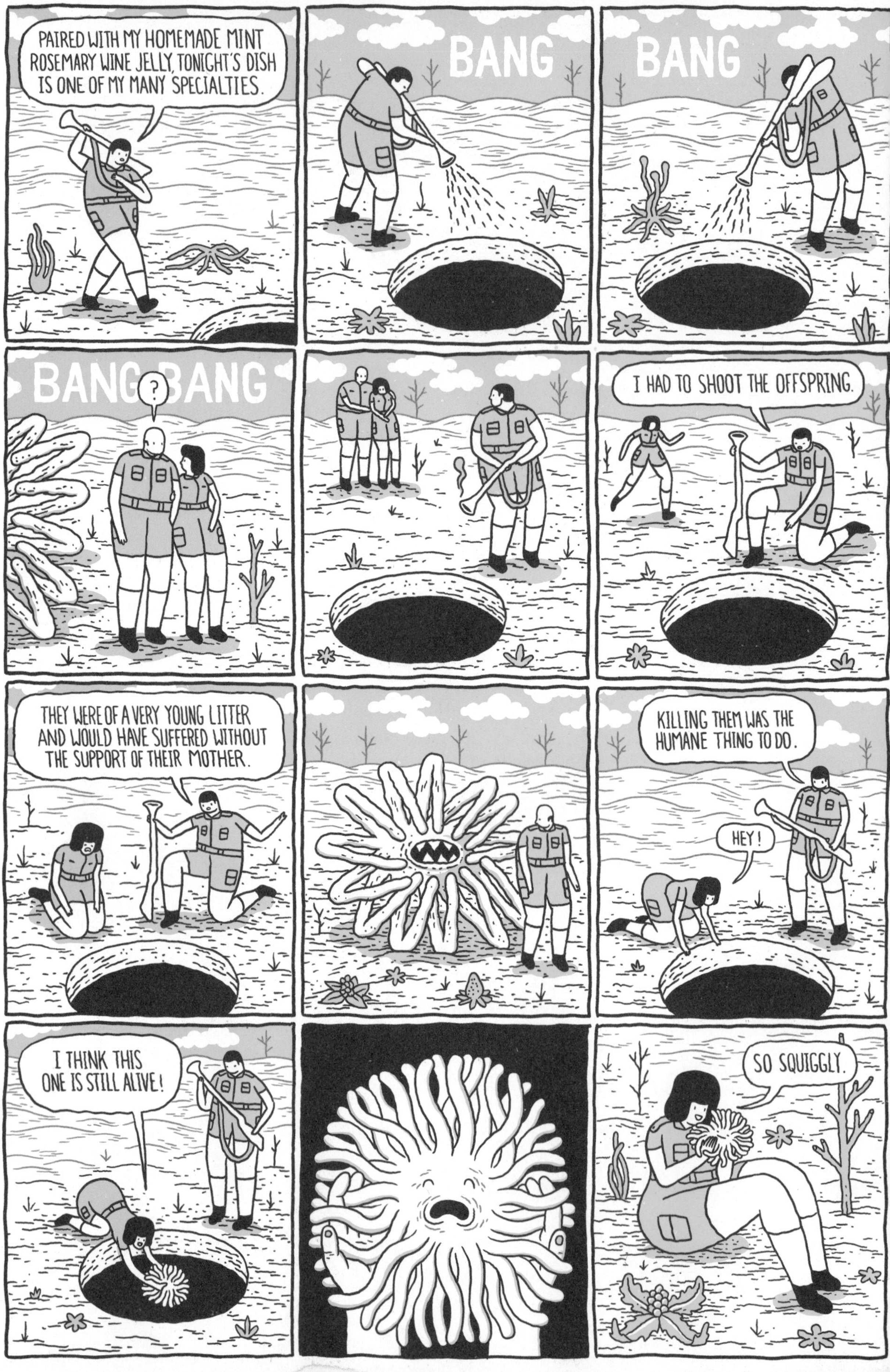
PAIRED WITH MY HOMEMADE MINT ROSEMARY WINE JELLY, TONIGHT'S DISH IS ONE OF MY MANY SPECIALTIES.
BANG
BANG
BANG
?
BANG
I HAD TO SHOOT THE OFFSPRING.
THEY WERE OF A VERY YOUNG LITTER AND WOULD HAVE SUFFERED WITHOUT THE SUPPORT OF THEIR MOTHER.
KILLING THEM WAS THE HUMANE THING TO DO.
HEY!
I THINK THIS ONE IS STILL ALIVE!
SO SQUIGGLY.

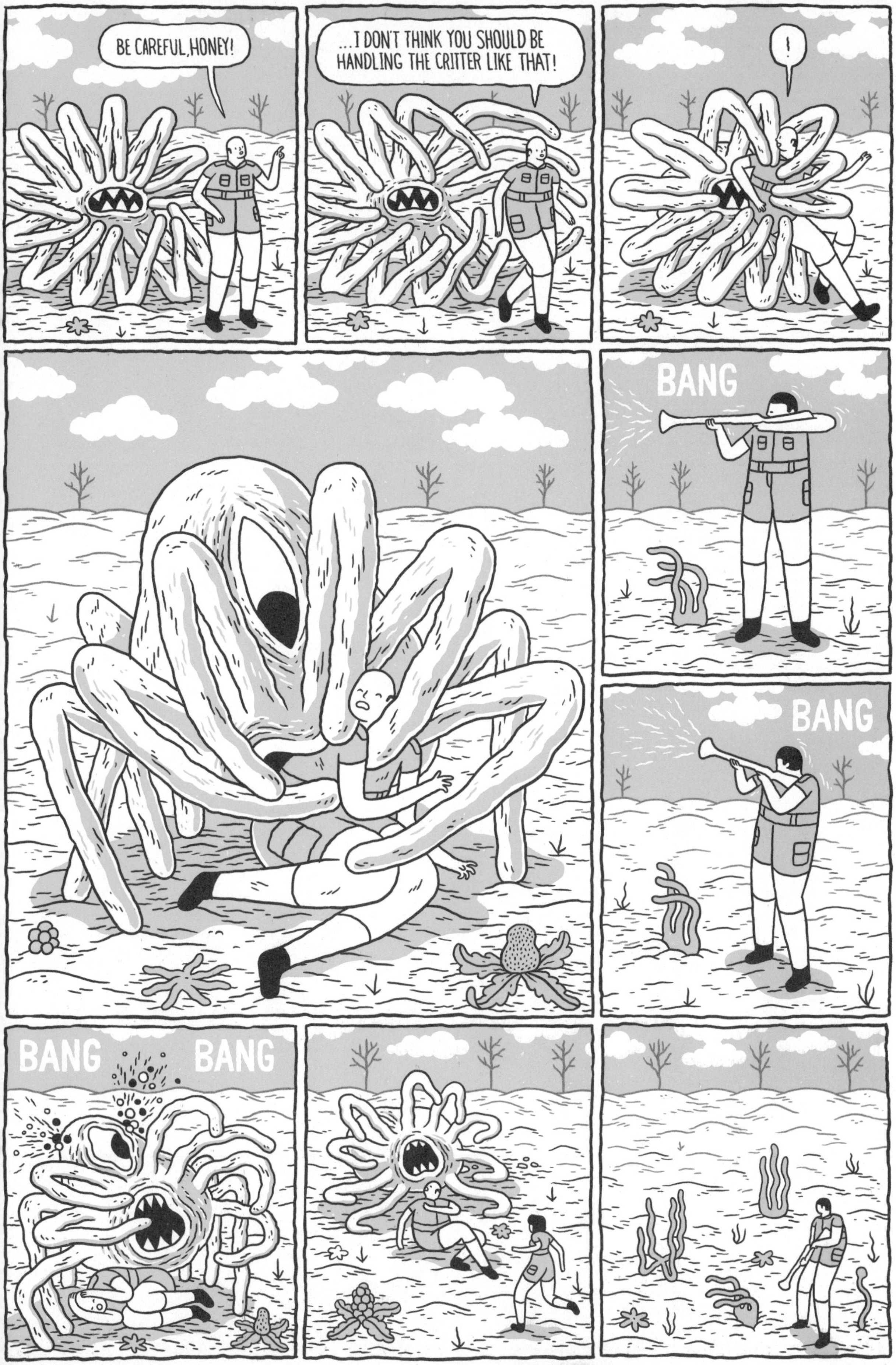
BE CAREFUL, HONEY!
...I DON'T THINK YOU SHOULD BE HANDLING THE CRITTER LIKE THAT!
!
BANG
BANG
BANG
BANG

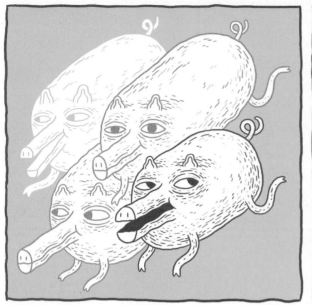

IT IS KNOWN OF THE DOMESTIC HOG THAT WITHIN WEEKS OF ITS RELEASE INTO THE WILD A DRASTIC TRANSFORMATION OCCURS.

IT'S AS IF, UPON BEING REUNITED WITH FRESH AIR AND OPEN SPACES, SOME LONG-FORGOTTEN CHROMOSOME IS REAWOKEN.

THE PIG GROWS LARGER AND HAIRIER.

IT BECOMES MORE AGGRESSIVE.

EVERYTHING, AT SOME POINT, IS REDUCED TO ITS MOST PRIMITIVE STATE.

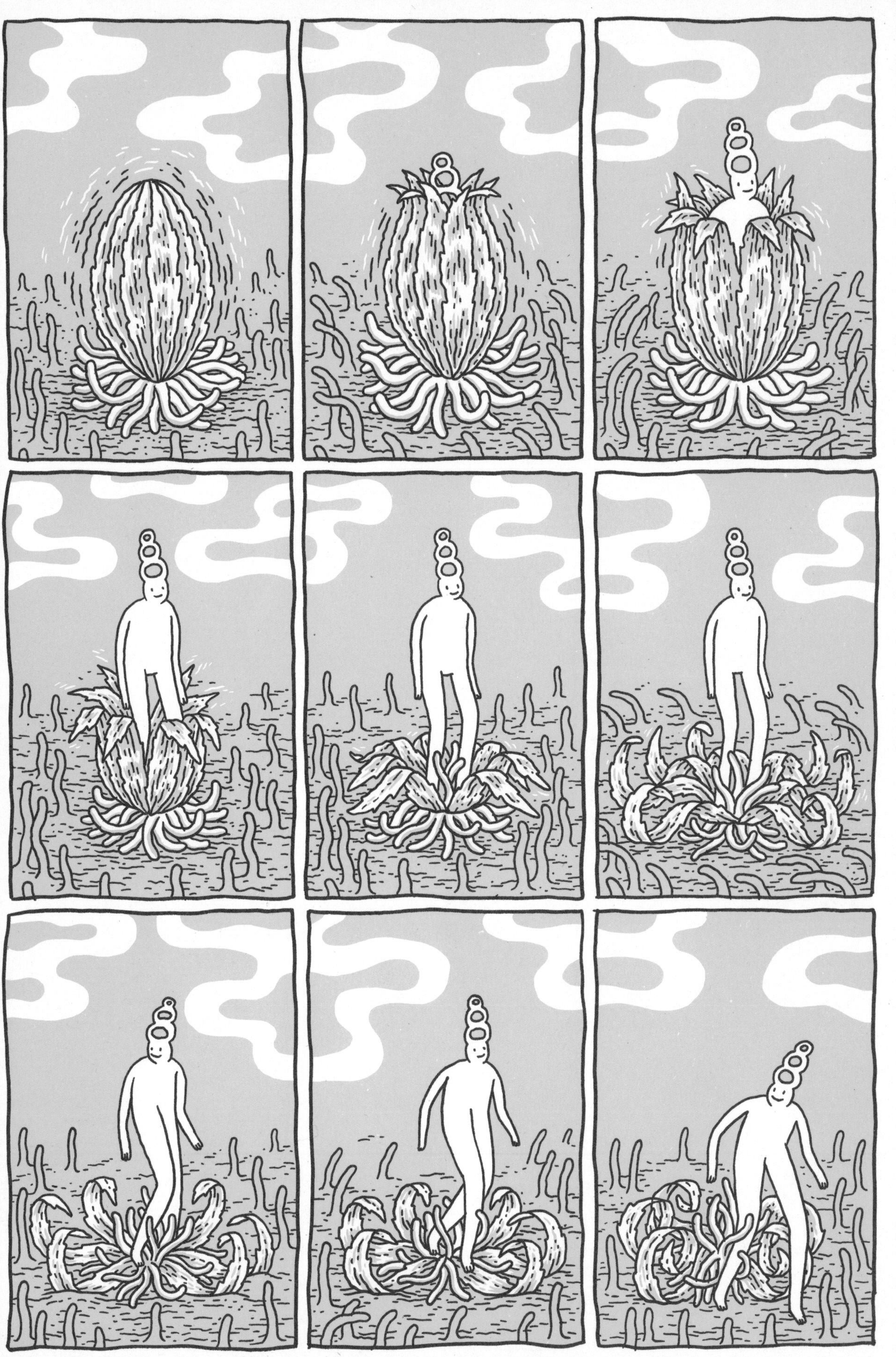

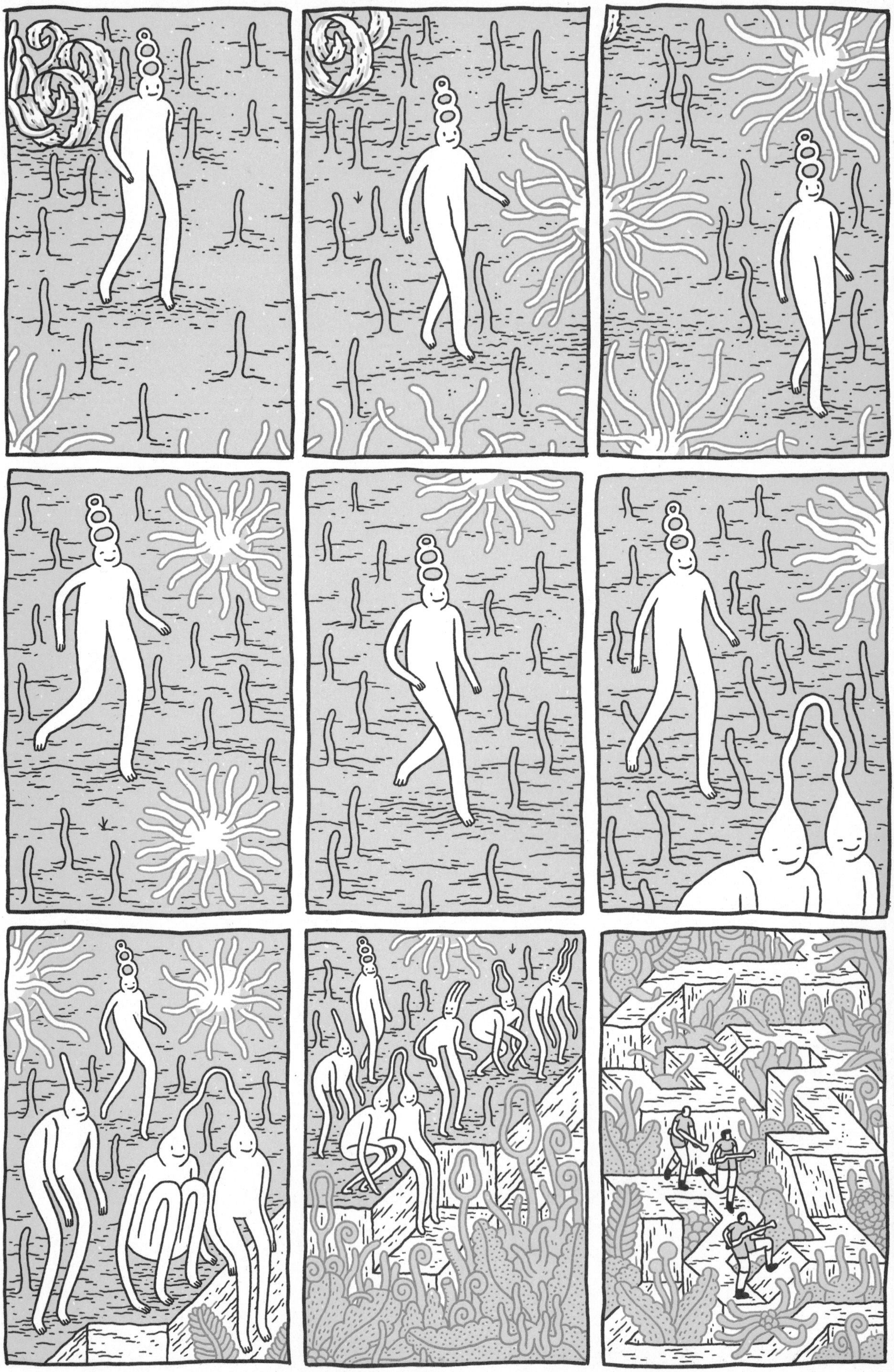

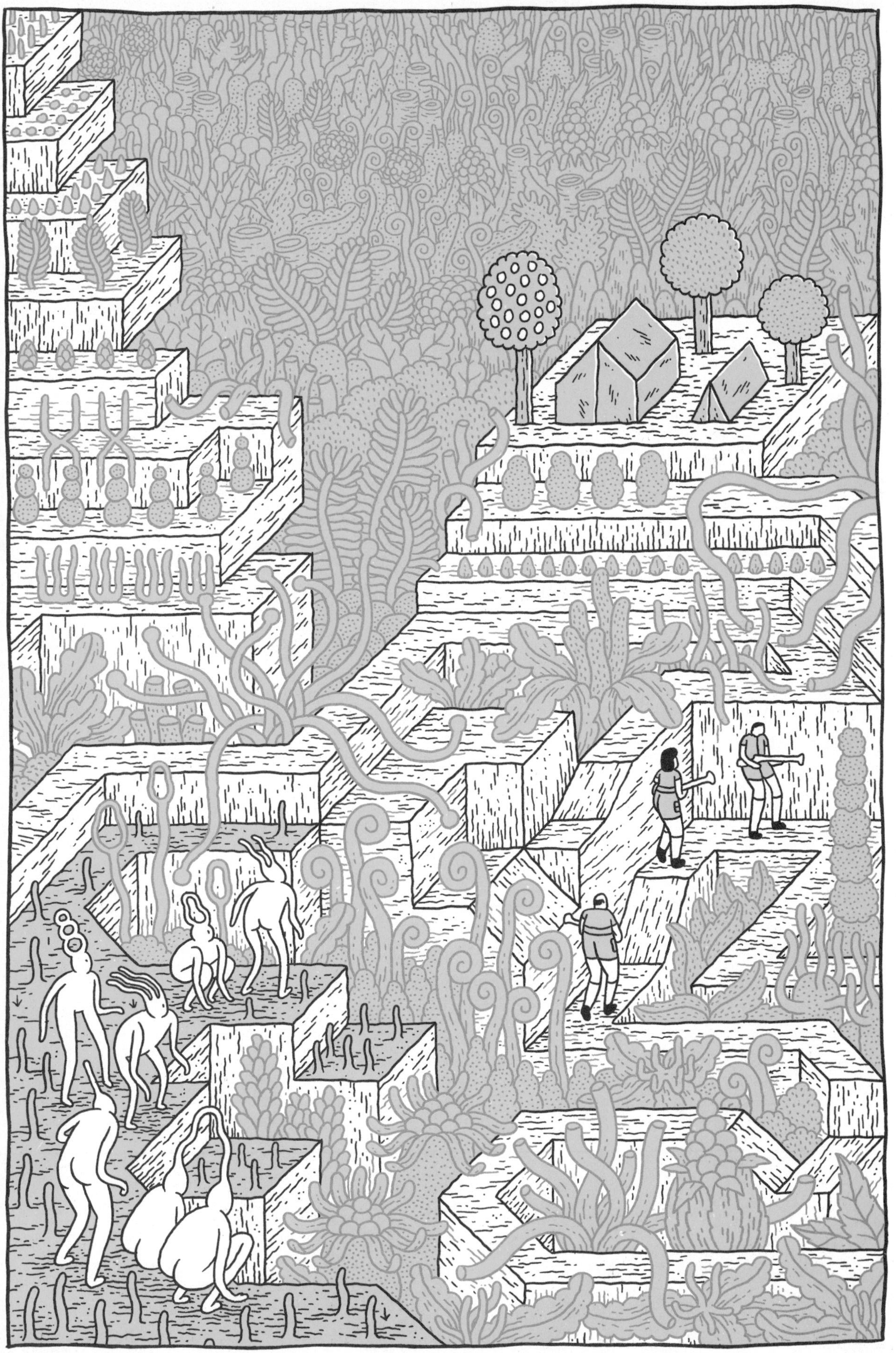

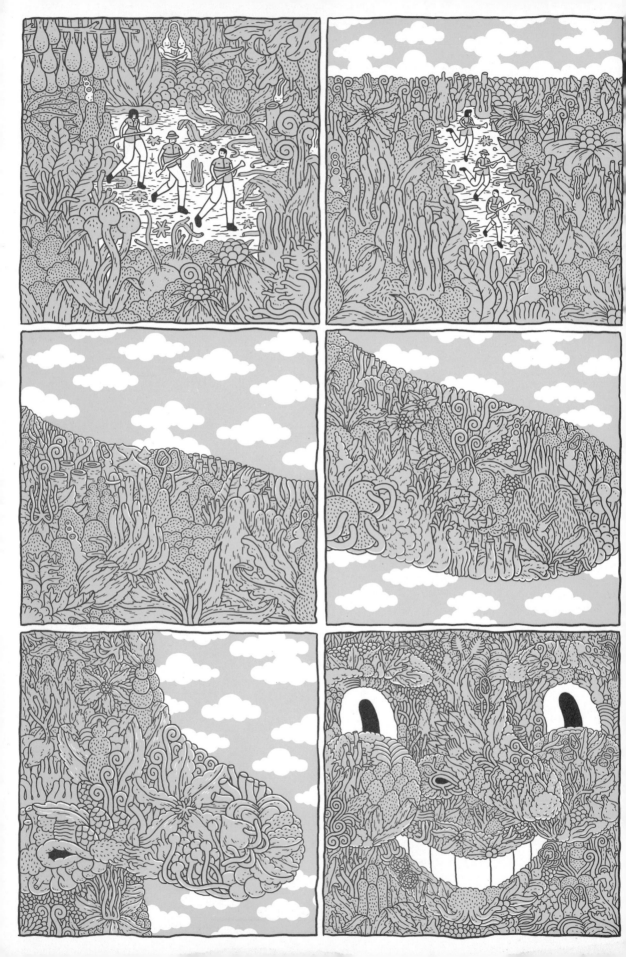

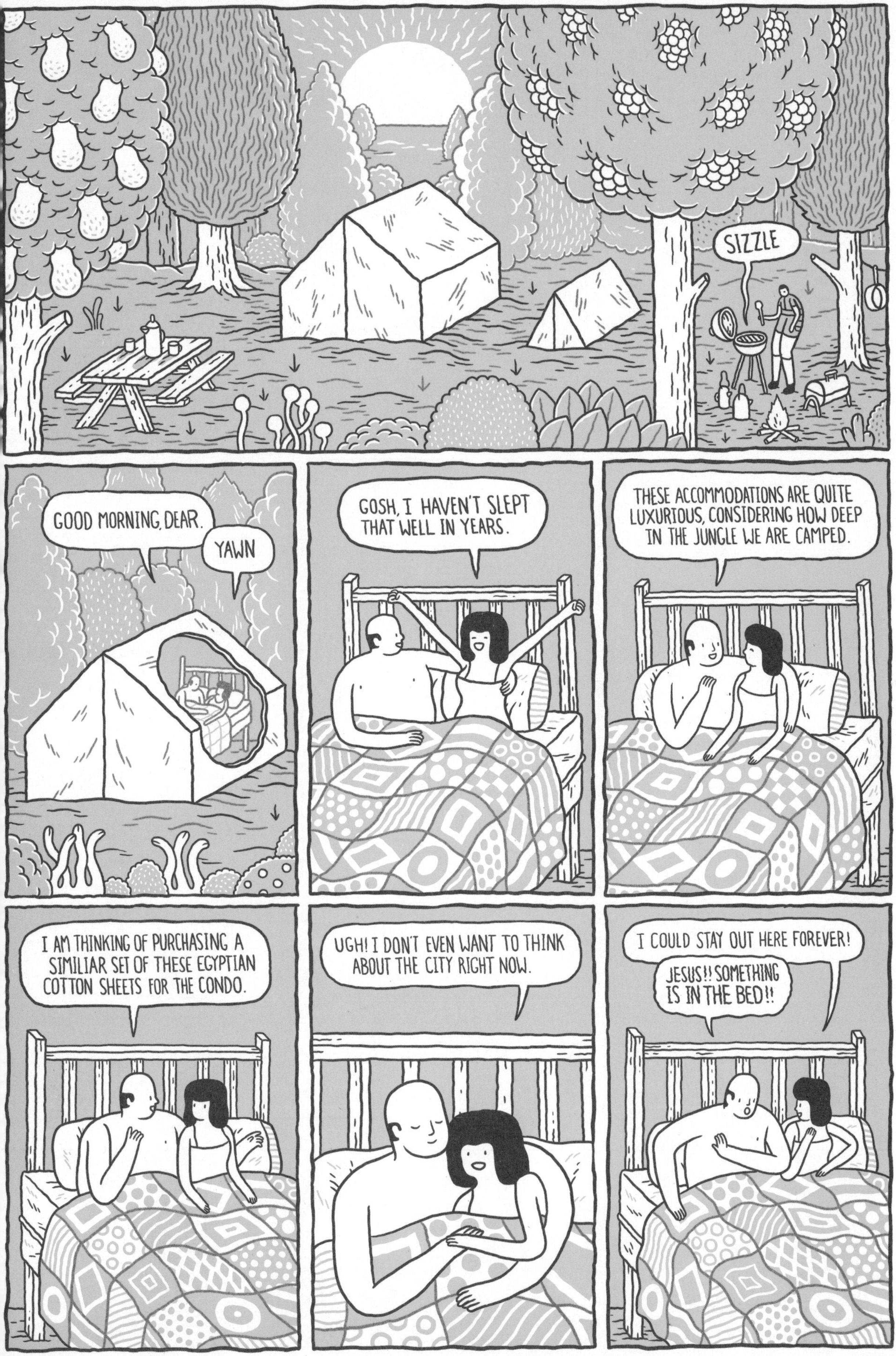
SIZZLE
GOOD MORNING, DEAR.
YAWN
GOSH, I HAVEN'T SLEPT THAT WELL IN YEARS.
THESE ACCOMMODATIONS ARE QUITE LUXURIOUS, CONSIDERING HOW DEEP IN THE JUNGLE WE ARE CAMPED.
I AM THINKING OF PURCHASING A SIMILIAR SET OF THESE EGYPTIAN COTTON SHEETS FOR THE CONDO.
UGH! I DON'T EVEN WANT TO THINK ABOUT THE CITY RIGHT NOW.
I COULD STAY OUT HERE FOREVER!
JESUS!! SOMETHING IS IN THE BED!!

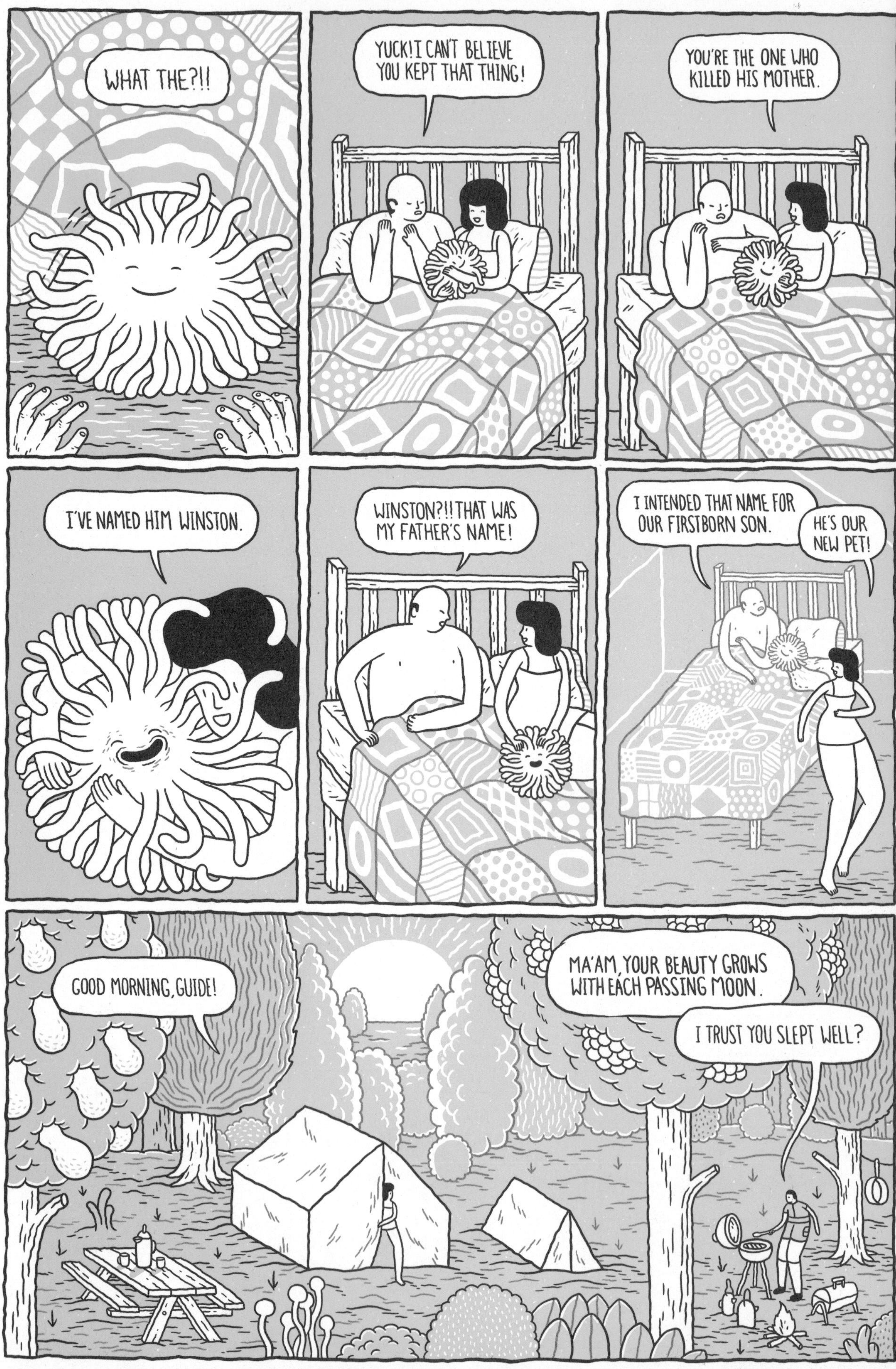
WHAT THE?!!
YUCK! I CAN'T BELIEVE YOU KEPT THAT THING!
YOU'RE THE ONE WHO KILLED HIS MOTHER.
I'VE NAMED HIM WINSTON.
WINSTON?!! THAT WAS MY FATHER'S NAME!
I INTENDED THAT NAME FOR OUR FIRSTBORN SON.
HE'S OUR NEW PET!
GOOD MORNING, GUIDE!
MA'AM, YOUR BEAUTY GROWS WITH EACH PASSING MOON.
I TRUST YOU SLEPT WELL?

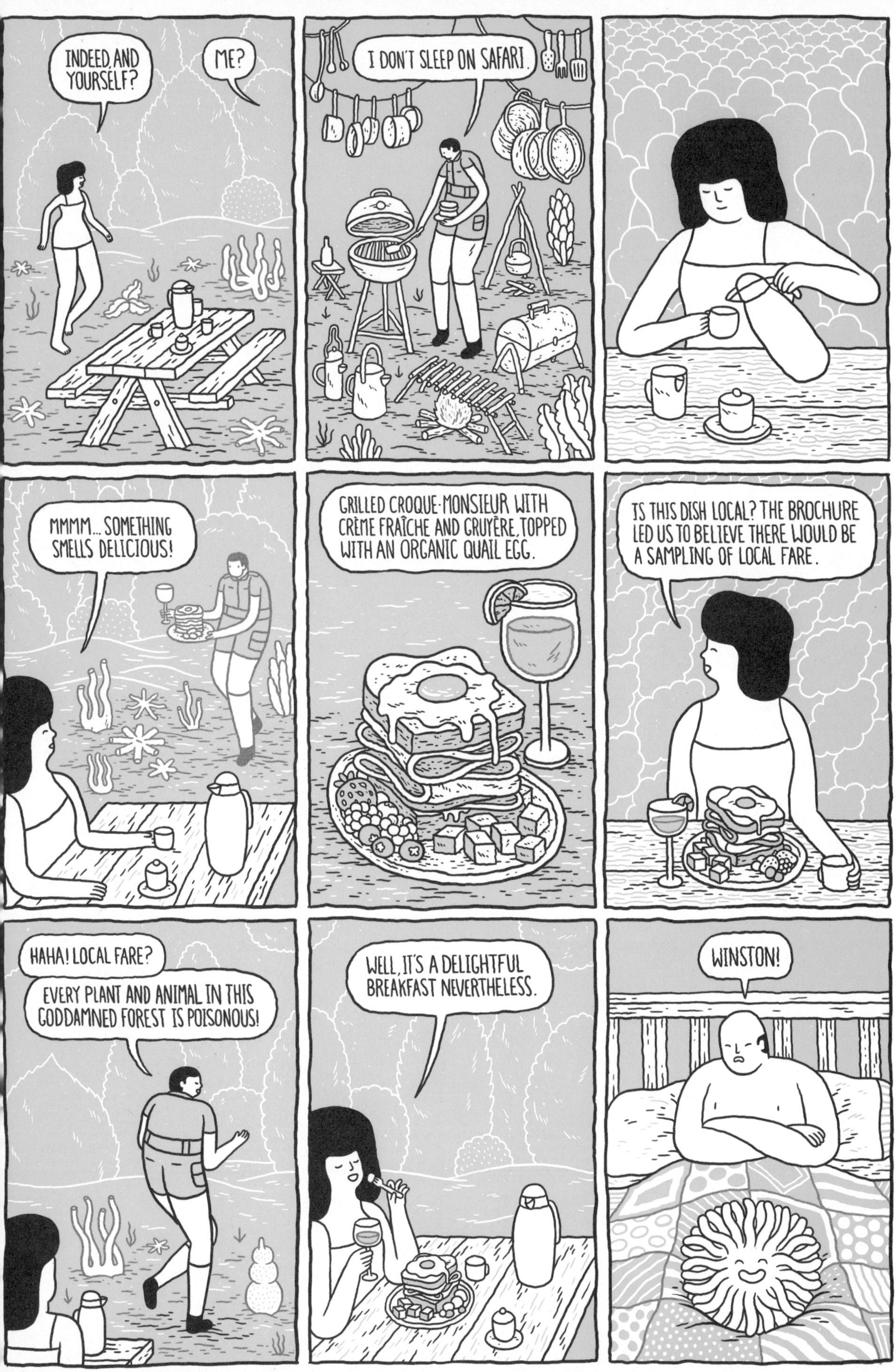
INDEED, AND YOURSELF?
ME?
I DON'T SLEEP ON SAFARI.
MMMM... SOMETHING SMELLS DELICIOUS!
GRILLED CROQUE-MONSIEUR WITH CRÈME FRAÎCHE AND GRUYÈRE, TOPPED WITH AN ORGANIC QUAIL EGG.
IS THIS DISH LOCAL? THE BROCHURE LED US TO BELIEVE THERE WOULD BE A SAMPLING OF LOCAL FARE.
HAHA! LOCAL FARE?
EVERY PLANT AND ANIMAL IN THIS GODDAMNED FOREST IS POISONOUS!
WELL, IT'S A DELIGHTFUL BREAKFAST NEVERTHELESS.
WINSTON!

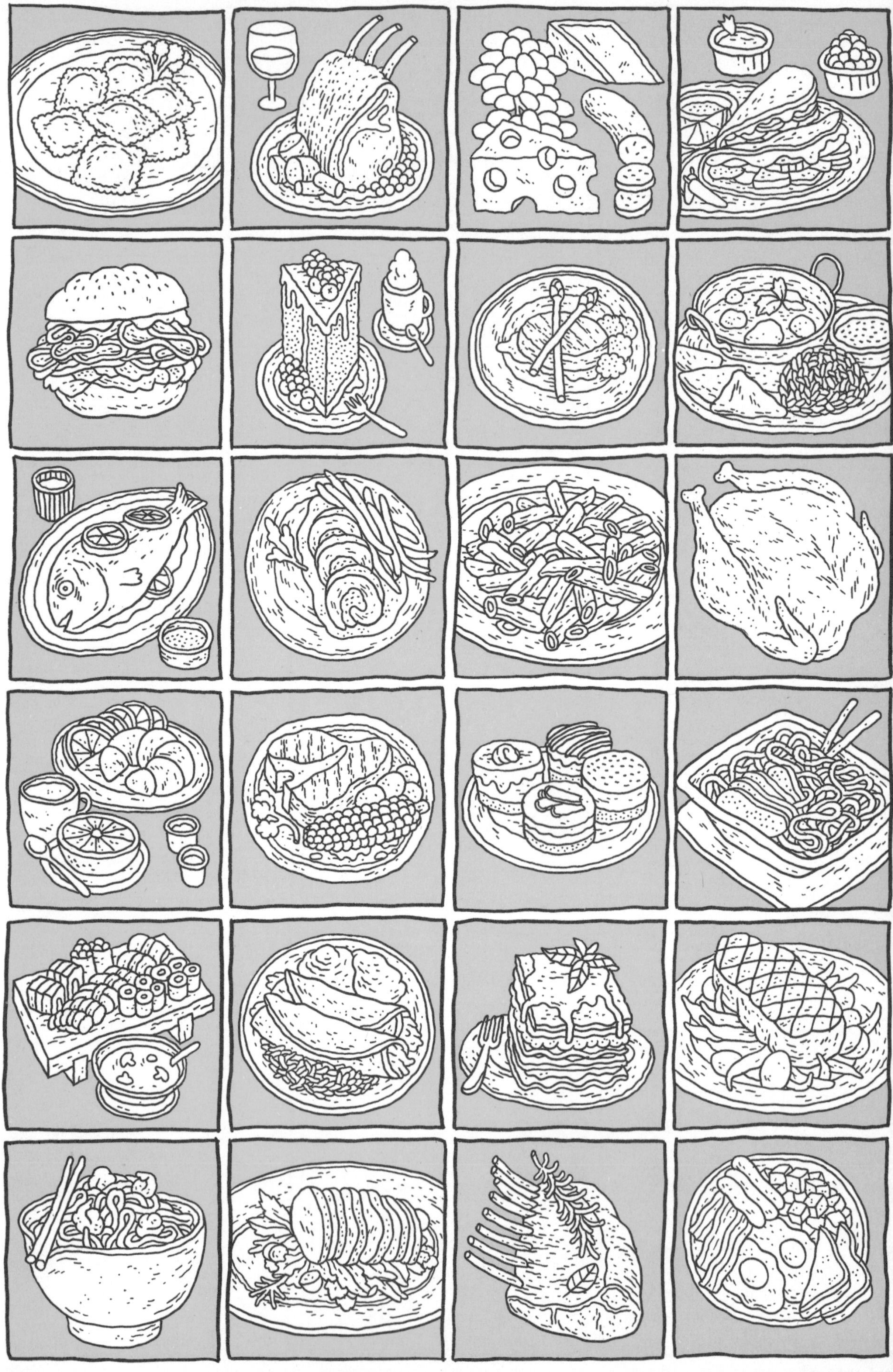

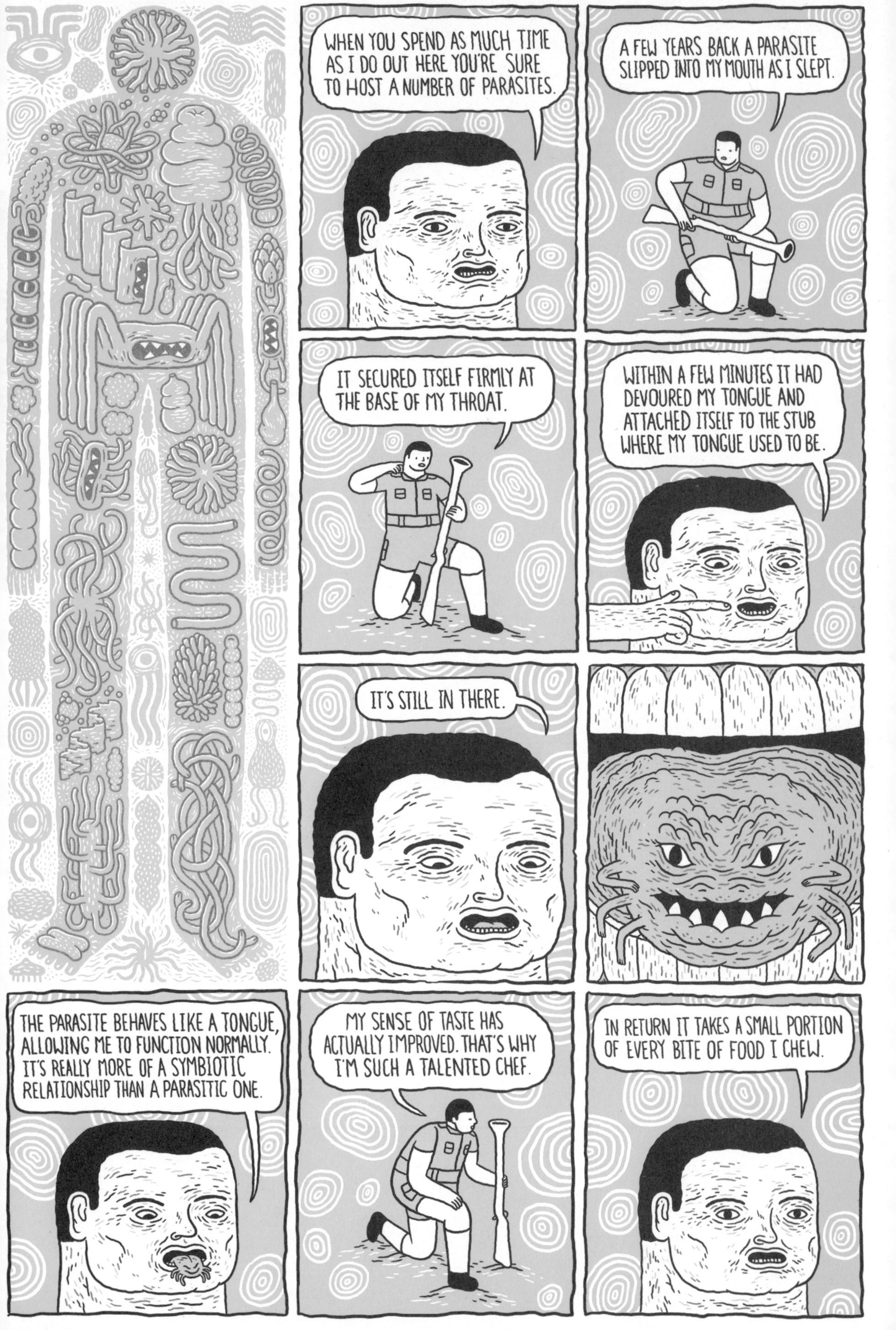
WHEN YOU SPEND AS MUCH TIME AS I DO OUT HERE YOU'RE SURE TO HOST A NUMBER OF PARASITES.
A FEW YEARS BACK A PARASITE SLIPPED INTO MY MOUTH AS I SLEPT.
IT SECURED ITSELF FIRMLY AT THE BASE OF MY THROAT.
WITHIN A FEW MINUTES IT HAD DEVOURED MY TONGUE AND ATTACHED ITSELF TO THE STUB WHERE MY TONGUE USED TO BE.
IT'S STILL IN THERE.
THE PARASITE BEHAVES LIKE A TONGUE, ALLOWING ME TO FUNCTION NORMALLY. IT'S REALLY MORE OF A SYMBIOTIC RELATIONSHIP THAN A PARASITIC ONE.
MY SENSE OF TASTE HAS ACTUALLY IMPROVED. THAT'S WHY I'M SUCH A TALENTED CHEF.
IN RETURN IT TAKES A SMALL PORTION OF EVERY BITE OF FOOD I CHEW.

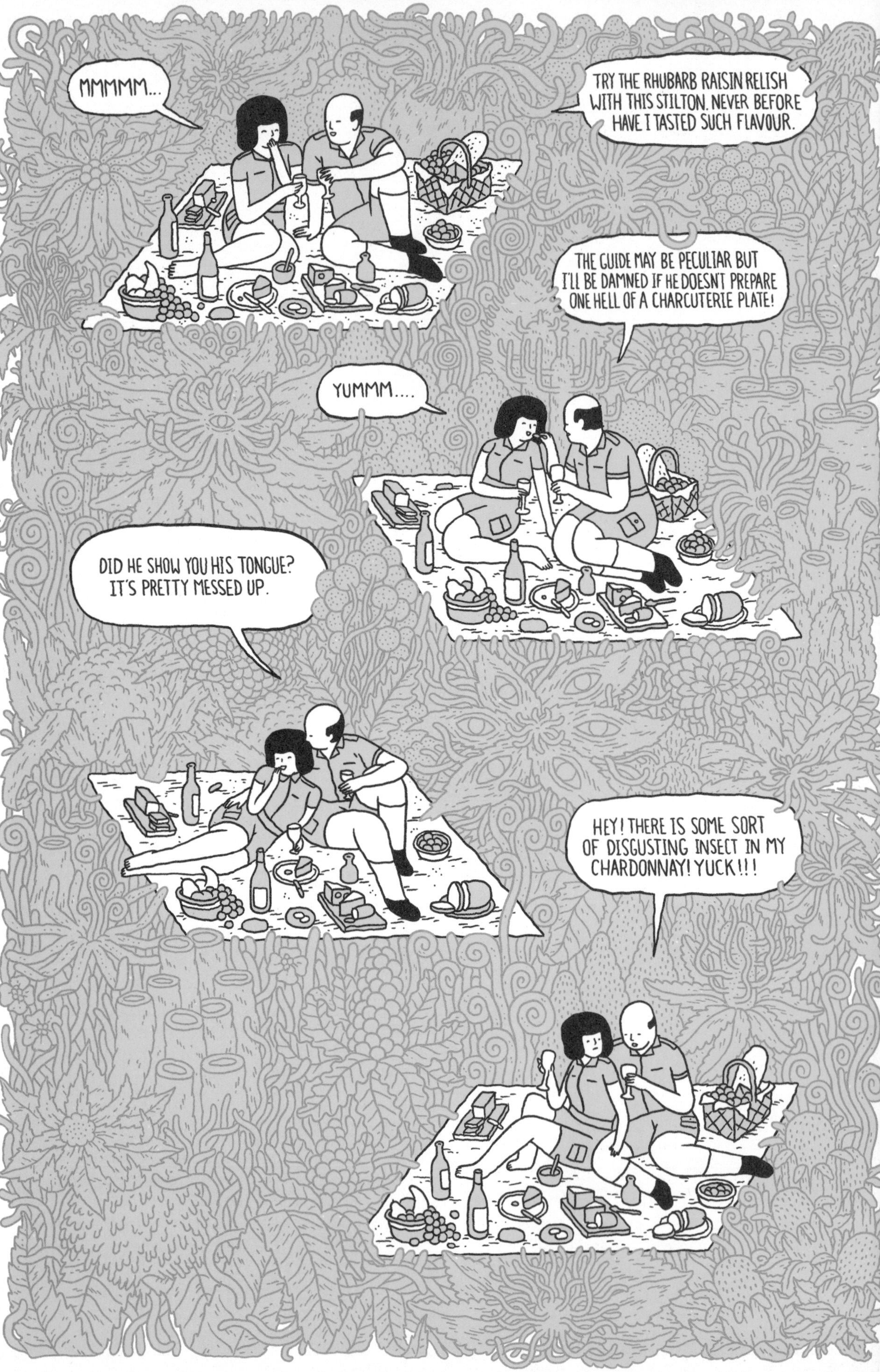

MMMMM...
TRY THE RHUBARB RAISIN RELISH WITH THIS STILTON. NEVER BEFORE HAVE I TASTED SUCH FLAVOUR.
THE GUIDE MAY BE PECULIAR BUT I'LL BE DAMNED IF HE DOESN'T PREPARE ONE HELL OF A CHARCUTERIE PLATE!
YUMMM....
DID HE SHOW YOU HIS TONGUE? IT'S PRETTY MESSED UP.
HEY! THERE IS SOME SORT OF DISGUSTING INSECT IN MY CHARDONNAY! YUCK!!!

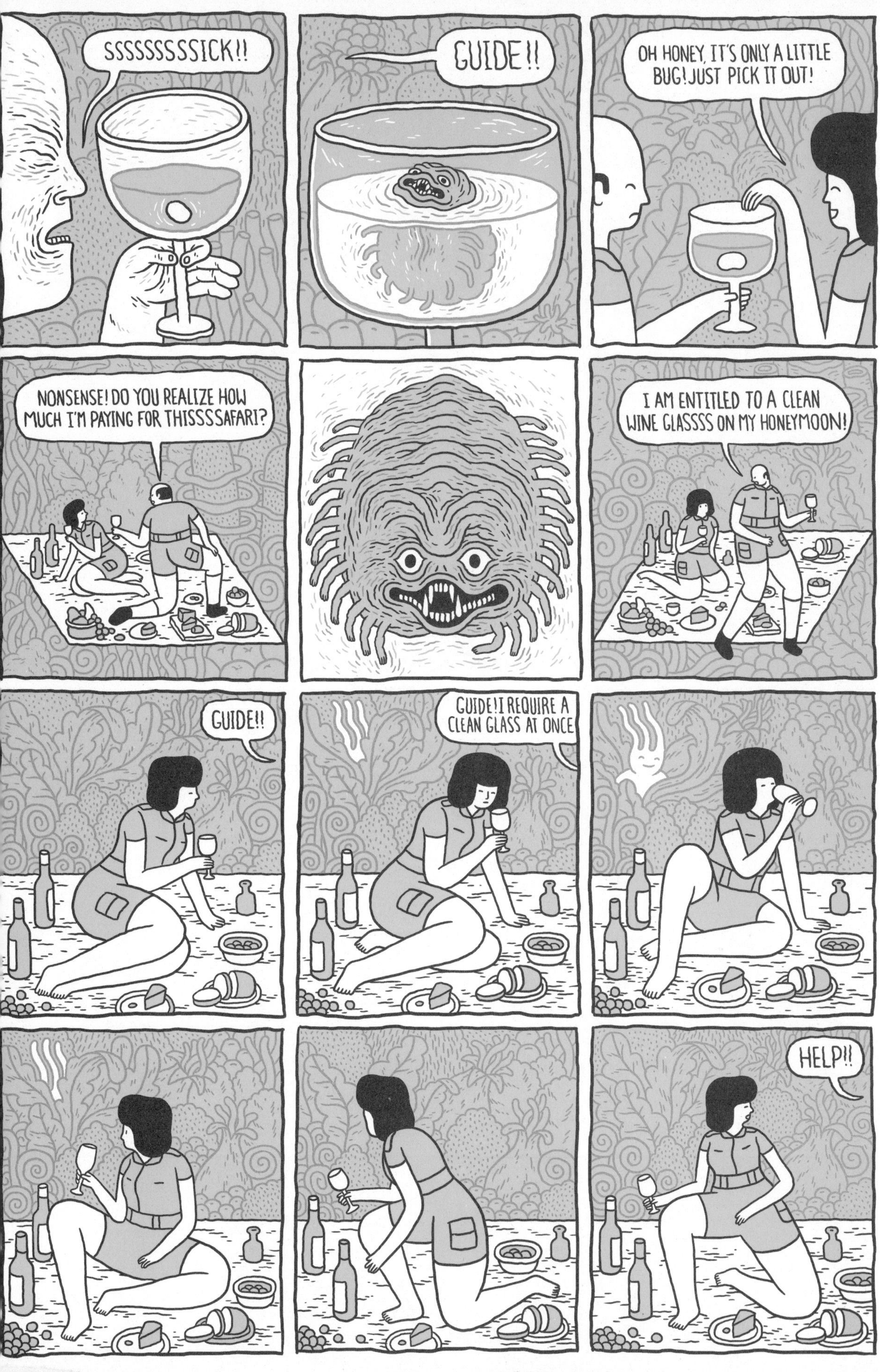
SSSSSSSSSICK!!
GUIDE!!
OH HONEY, IT'S ONLY A LITTLE BUG! JUST PICK IT OUT!
NONSENSE! DO YOU REALIZE HOW MUCH I'M PAYING FOR THISSSSAFARI?
I AM ENTITLED TO A CLEAN WINE GLASSSS ON MY HONEYMOON!
GUIDE!!
GUIDE! I REQUIRE A CLEAN GLASS AT ONCE
HELP!!

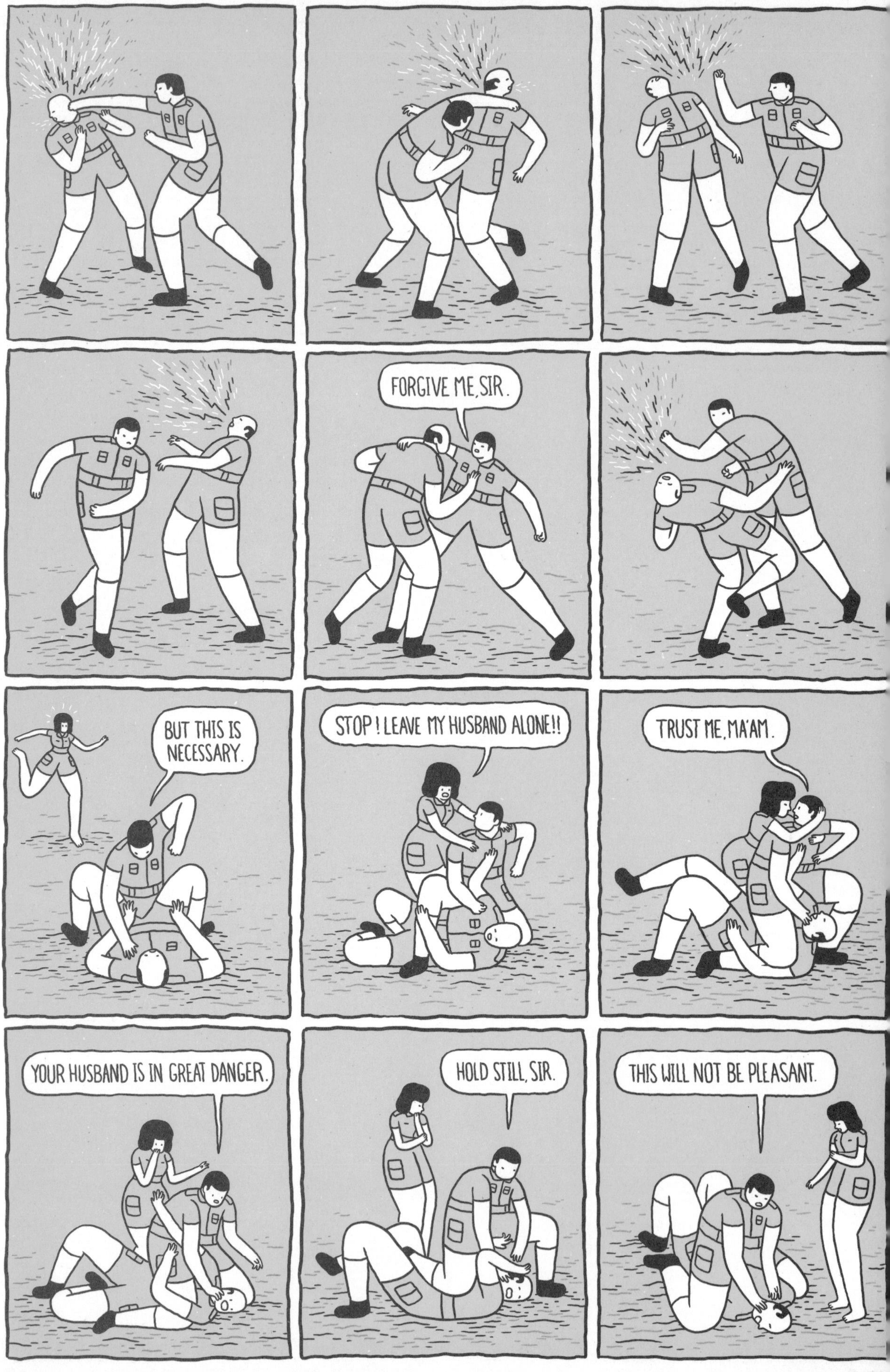
FORGIVE ME, SIR.
BUT THIS IS NECESSARY.
STOP! LEAVE MY HUSBAND ALONE!!
TRUST ME, MA'AM.
YOUR HUSBAND IS IN GREAT DANGER.
HOLD STILL, SIR.
THIS WILL NOT BE PLEASANT.

SSSSS
GOT IT!
SSSSSSS
SSSSSSSS
SSSSS
SSSSS
SSSS
SORRY ABOUT THE BEATING, SIR.
SSSSS
REPETITIVE HEAD TRAUMA IS THE SAFEST METHOD OF DISLODGING A PARASITE.
JESUS!
HOW THE HELL DID THAT THING GET INSIDE OF ME?
THOUGH IT PREFERS THE EAR CANAL, THE CREATURE WILL PENETRATE ANY ORIFICE.
MOST LIKELY, IT PASSED THROUGH YOUR RECTUM WHILE YOU SLEPT.
SSSSSS
HAVE YOU FOLKS BEEN WEARING YOUR BUTT PLUGS?

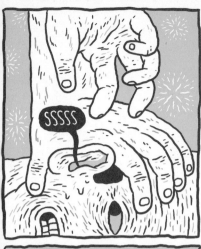

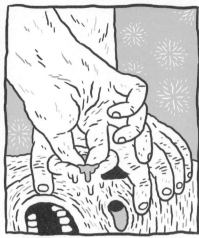

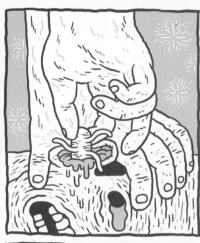

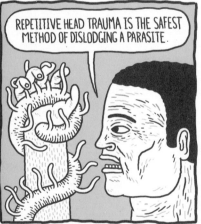

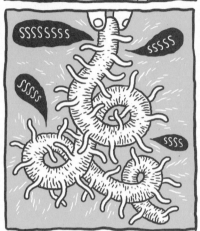

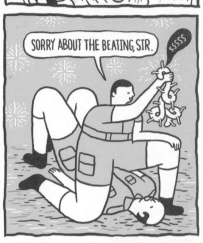

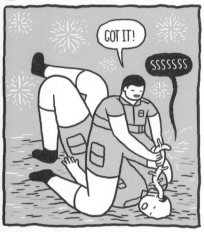

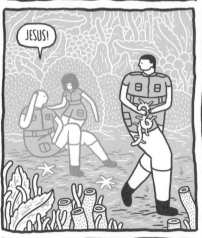

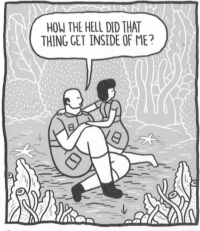

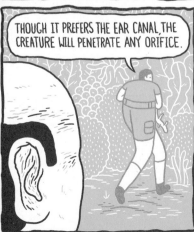

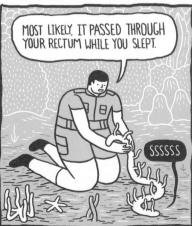

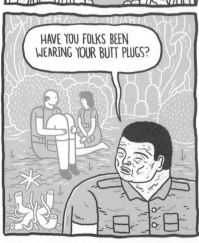

ONCE INSIDE, THE LEECH COILS ITSELF AROUND THE BRAIN AND FEEDS UPON YOUR SOUL.

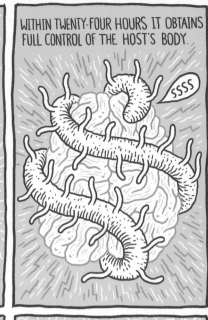

WITHIN TWENTY-FOUR HOURS IT OBTAINS FULL CONTROL OF THE HOST'S BODY.

SSS

THIS REGION IS TEEMING WITH SUCH HATEFUL PARASITES!

HALF THE ANIMALS IN THIS JUNGLE ARE INFECTED!

THAT IS WHY THIS IS A DANGEROUS TOURIST DESTINATION.

BOOM BOOM

BOOM

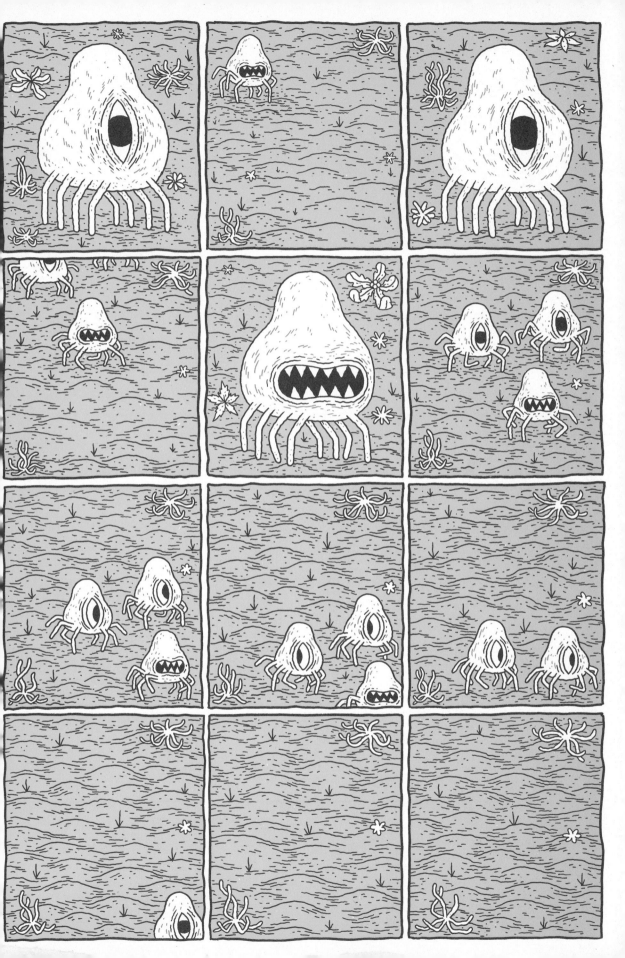

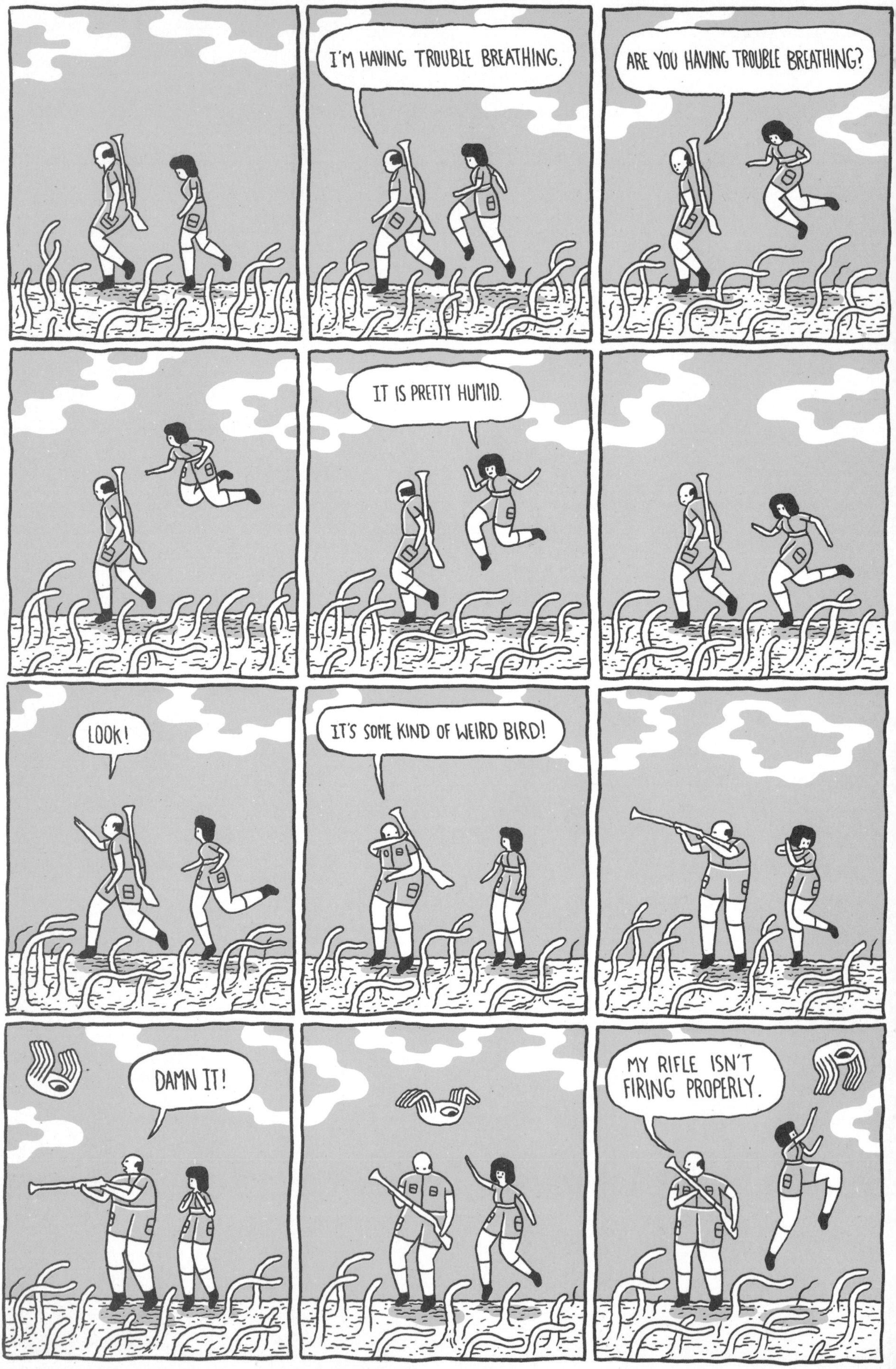
I'M HAVING TROUBLE BREATHING.
ARE YOU HAVING TROUBLE BREATHING?
IT IS PRETTY HUMID.
LOOK!
IT'S SOME KIND OF WEIRD BIRD!
DAMN IT!
MY RIFLE ISN'T FIRING PROPERLY.

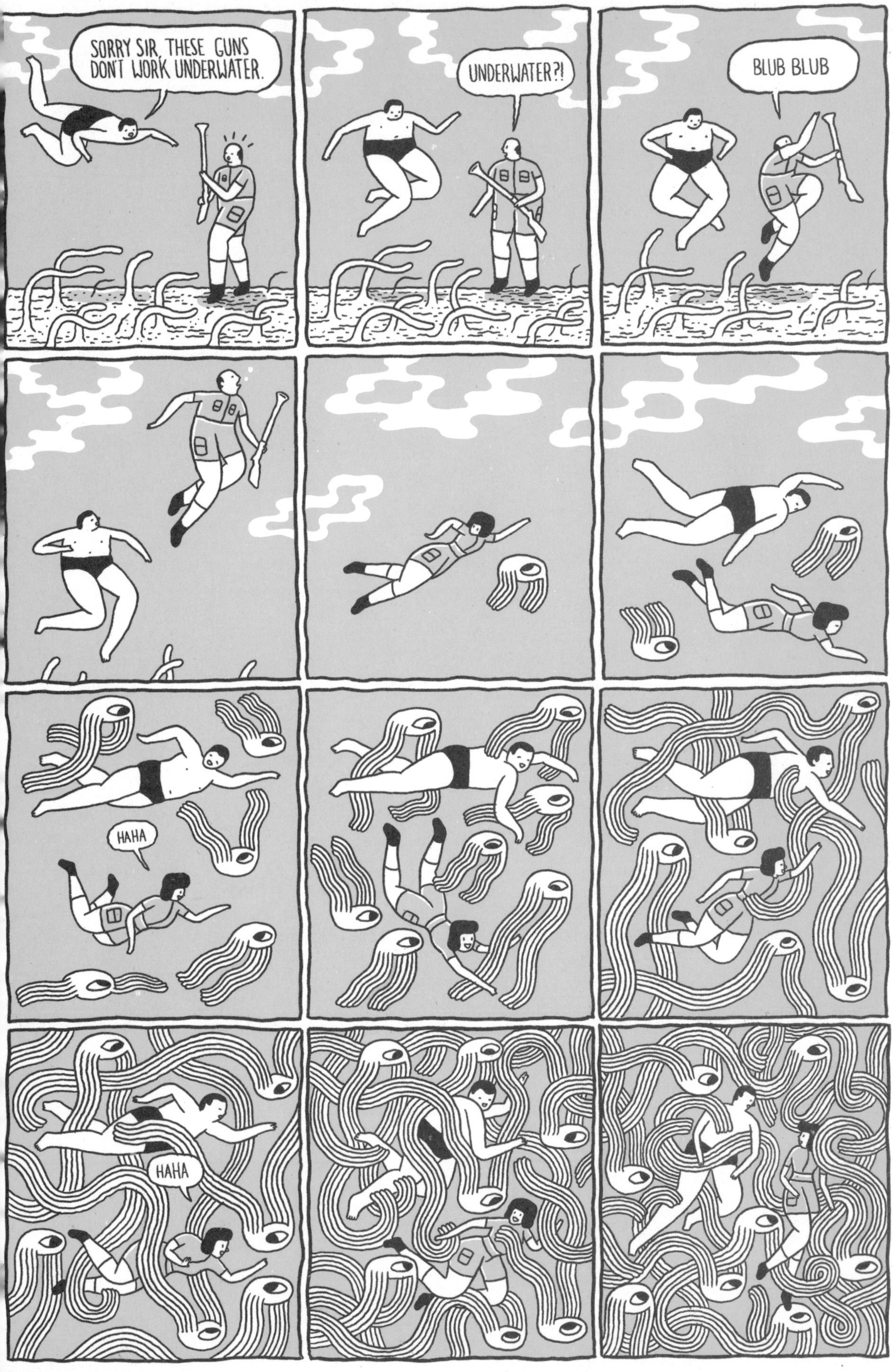
SORRY SIR, THESE GUNS DON'T WORK UNDERWATER.
UNDERWATER?!
BLUB BLUB
HAHA
HAHA

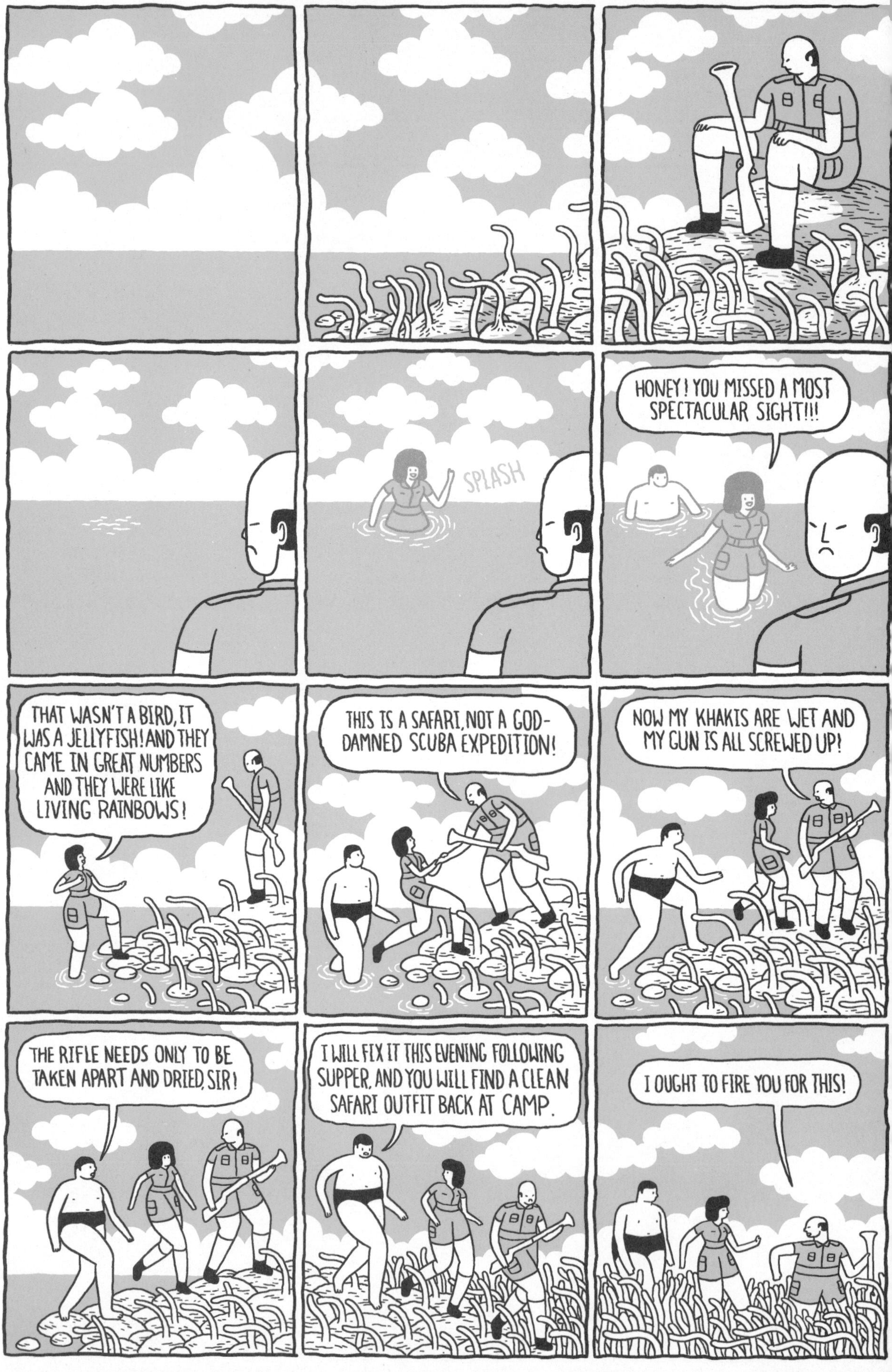
SPLASH
HONEY! YOU MISSED A MOST SPECTACULAR SIGHT!!!
THAT WASN'T A BIRD, IT WAS A JELLYFISH! AND THEY CAME IN GREAT NUMBERS AND THEY WERE LIKE LIVING RAINBOWS!
THIS IS A SAFARI, NOT A GOD-DAMNED SCUBA EXPEDITION!
NOW MY KHAKIS ARE WET AND MY GUN IS ALL SCREWED UP!
THE RIFLE NEEDS ONLY TO BE TAKEN APART AND DRIED, SIR!
I WILL FIX IT THIS EVENING FOLLOWING SUPPER, AND YOU WILL FIND A CLEAN SAFARI OUTFIT BACK AT CAMP.
I OUGHT TO FIRE YOU FOR THIS!

THE FIRST SYMPTOM OF INFECTION IS
AN INTENSE EXPLOSION OF HUNGER

IN AN EFFORT TO FATTEN ITS HOST, THE
PARASITE NEUROLOGICALLY INHIBITS
THE AREA OF THE BRAIN THAT GIVES
ONE THE SENSATION OF FEELING FULL.

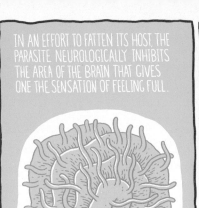

THE INFECTED ORGANISM BECOMES EXTREMELY
AGGRESSIVE AND PREDATORY, HUNTING
AND DEVOURING EVERY ANIMAL AVAILABLE.

AFTER SEVERAL WEEKS OF EXCESSIVE
GORGING THE HOST IS PROMPTED TO
CLIMB THE TALLEST TREE IN THE REGION.

IT IS UPON THE HIGHEST BRANCHES THAT
THE COCOONING PROCESS IS INITIATED.

A THICK ACIDIC SUBSTANCE IS EXCRETED
FROM THE INFECTED CREATURE'S PORES,
ENVELOPING ITS ENTIRE BODY IN
A STICKY PROTECTIVE CASING.

WITHIN THE COCOON THE BODY IS
REDUCED TO A POOL OF LIQUID ORGANIC
MATTER, PROVIDING NOURISHMENT TO
A PULSING MASS OF GESTATING LARVAE.

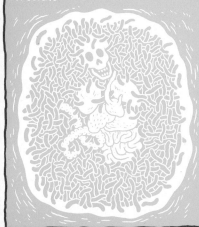

UPON COMPLETION OF THE PUPAL
STAGE, AFTER CONSUMING THE ENTIRETY
OF THE HOST'S CARCASS, THE NEWLY
FORMED CREATURES BEGIN TO EMERGE.

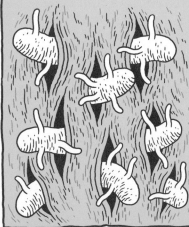

THE YOUNG PARASITES ERUPT FROM THE
COCOON WITH GREAT FEROCITY, RAINING
DOWN UPON THE FOREST FLOOR AND
SCATTERING WILDLY IN ALL DIRECTIONS.

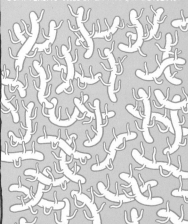

WITHIN THE LIGHT GROWS A FOREST SO DEEP AND SPRAWLING THAT ITS EXISTENCE CANNOT BE CONTAINED BY THE PHYSICAL WORLD.

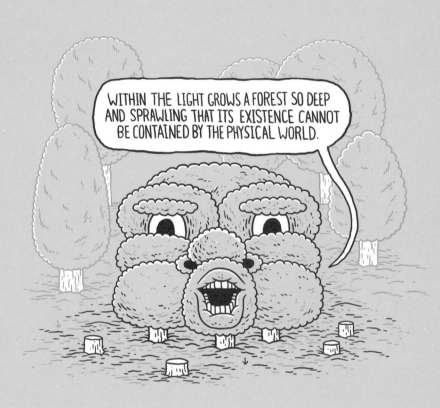

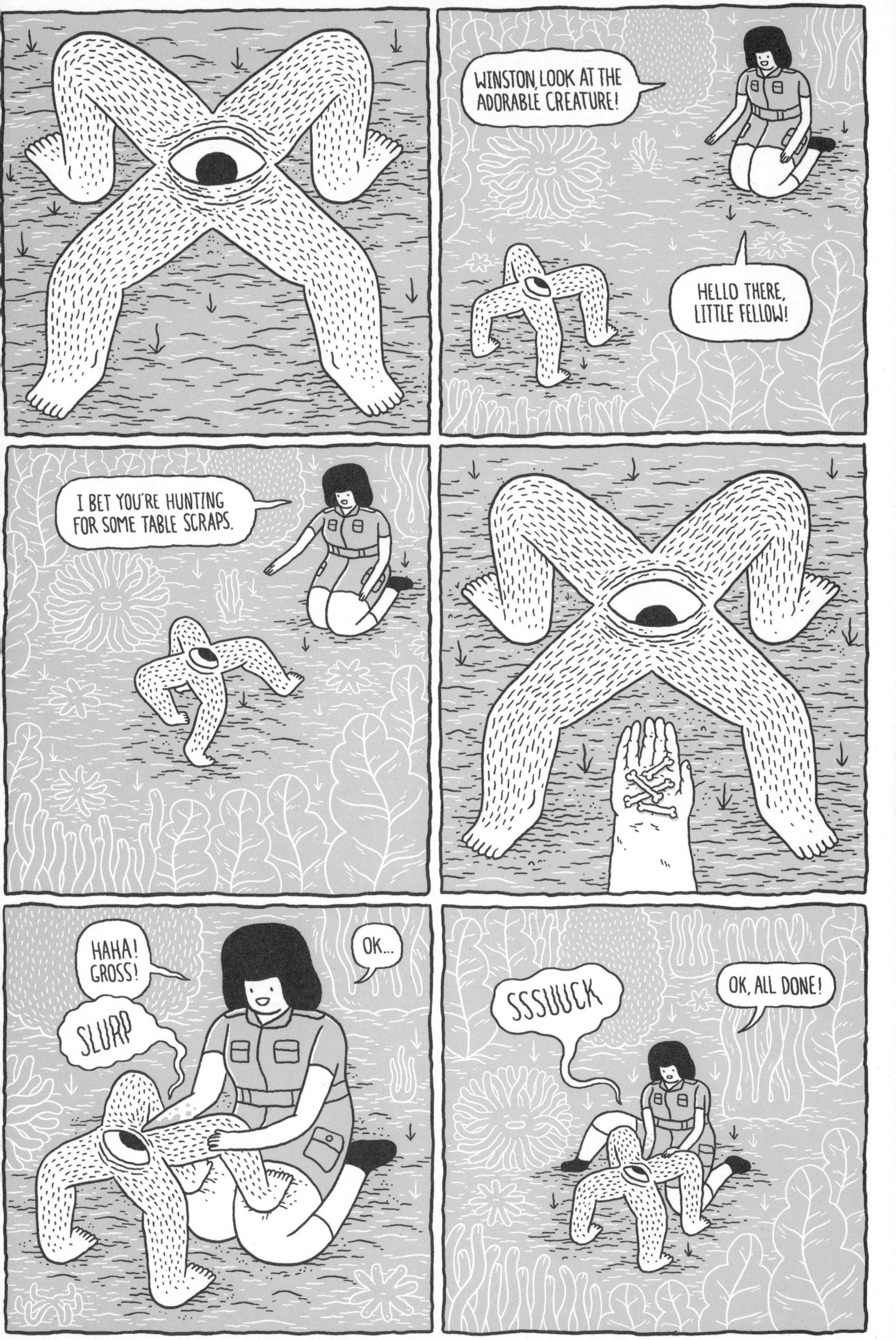
WINSTON, LOOK AT THE ADORABLE CREATURE!
HELLO THERE, LITTLE FELLOW!
I BET YOU'RE HUNTING FOR SOME TABLE SCRAPS.
HAHA! GROSS!
OK...
SLURP
SSSUUCK
OK, ALL DONE!

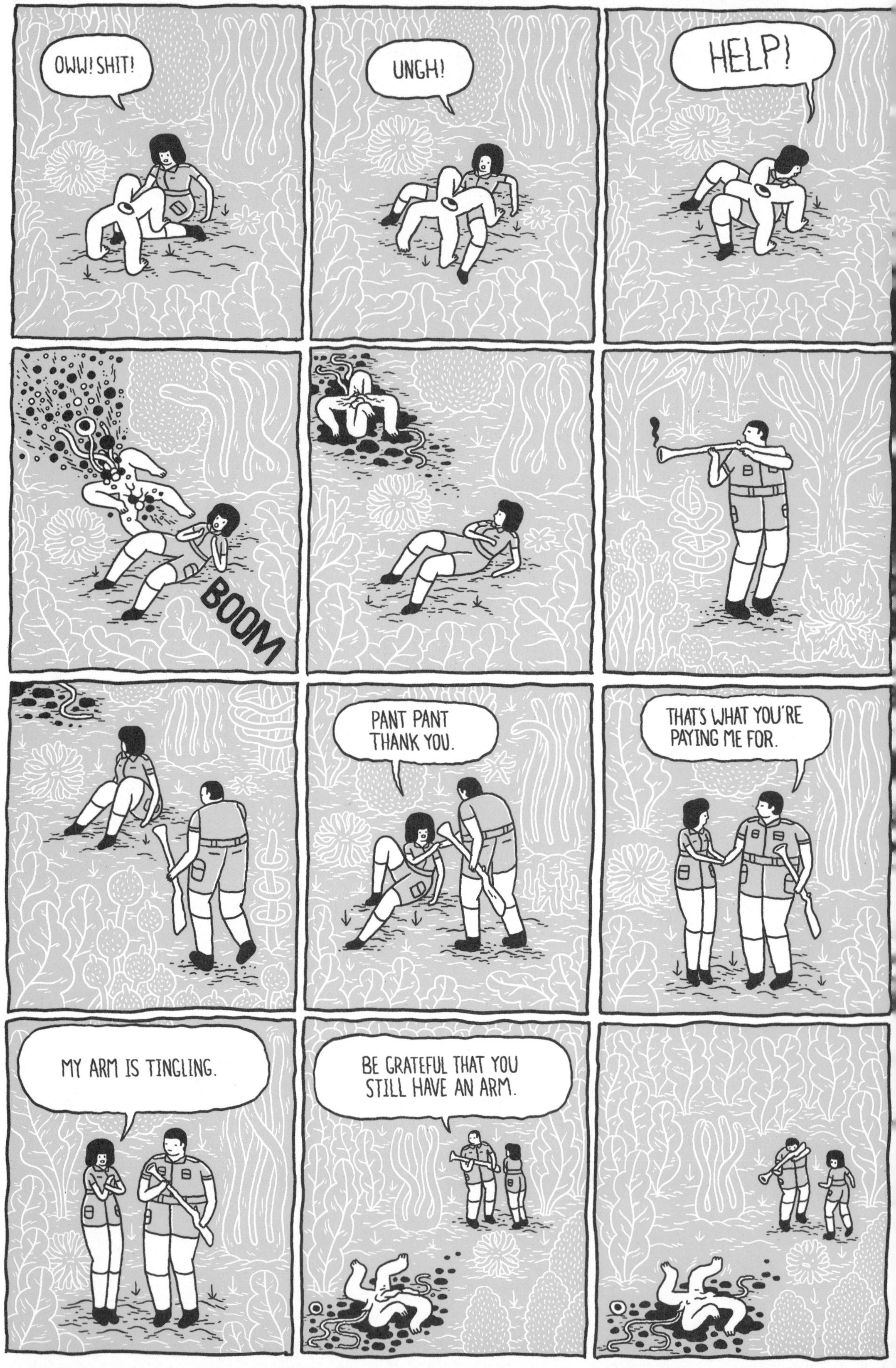
OWW! SHIT!
UNGH!
HELP!
BOOM
PANT PANT THANK YOU.
THAT'S WHAT YOU'RE PAYING ME FOR.
MY ARM IS TINGLING.
BE GRATEFUL THAT YOU STILL HAVE AN ARM.

YOU BEST HEAD ON BACK TO CAMP FOR BREAKFAST.

I MUST APOLOGIZE FOR MY HUSBAND'S BEHAVIOUR.

BACK IN THE CITY HE IS A VERY POWERFUL MAN, AND UNACCUSTOMED TO APPEARING VULNERABLE.

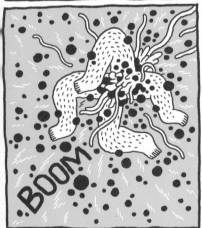

I HAVE PREPARED AN ASSORTMENT OF CROISSANTS AND FRESH FRUITS.

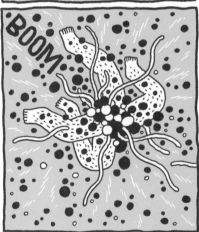

A SELECTION OF SPECIALTY COFFEES ARE ALSO AVAILABLE.

I PREFER THE VANILLA HAZELNUT BLEND, MYSELF.

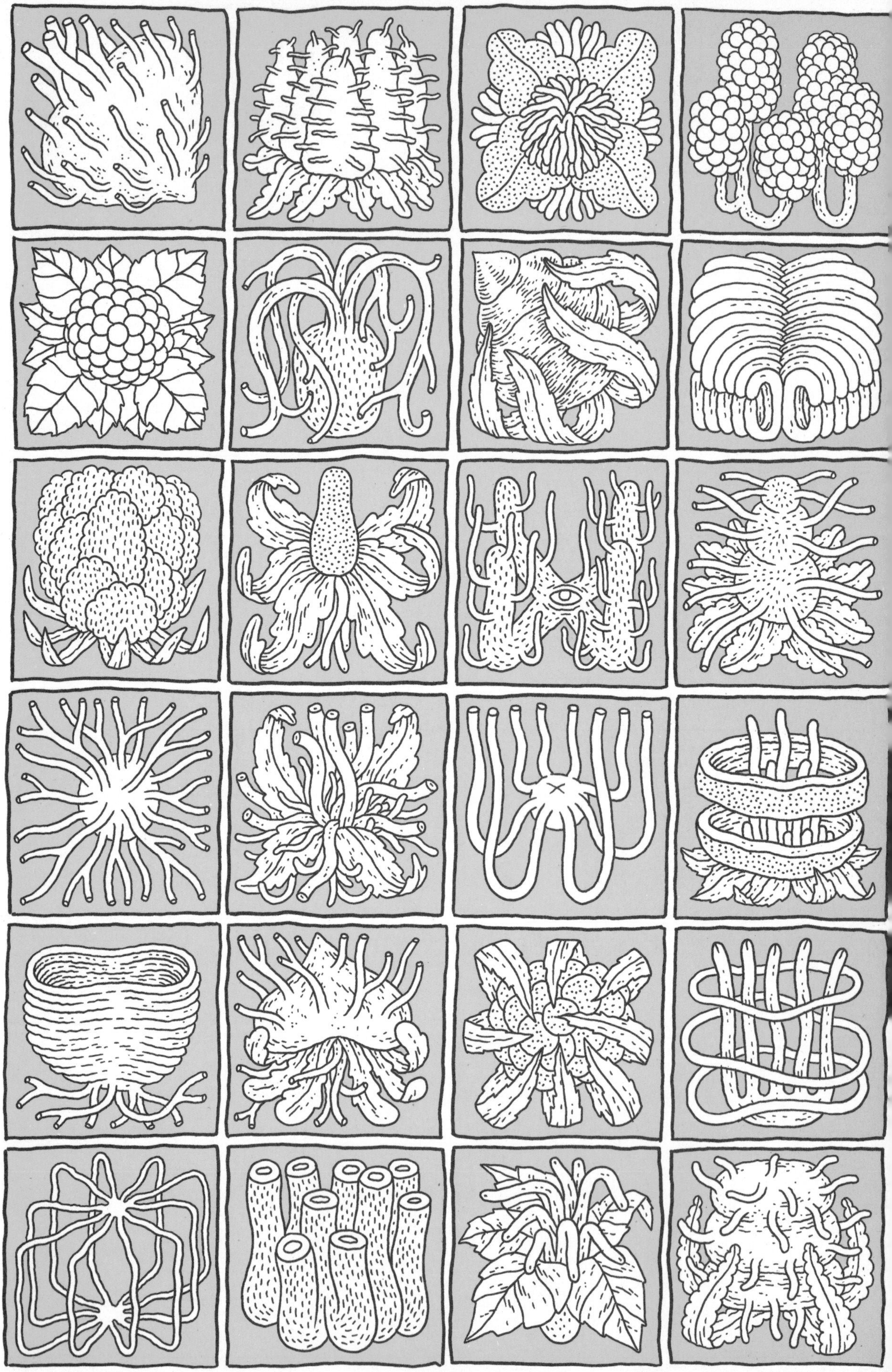

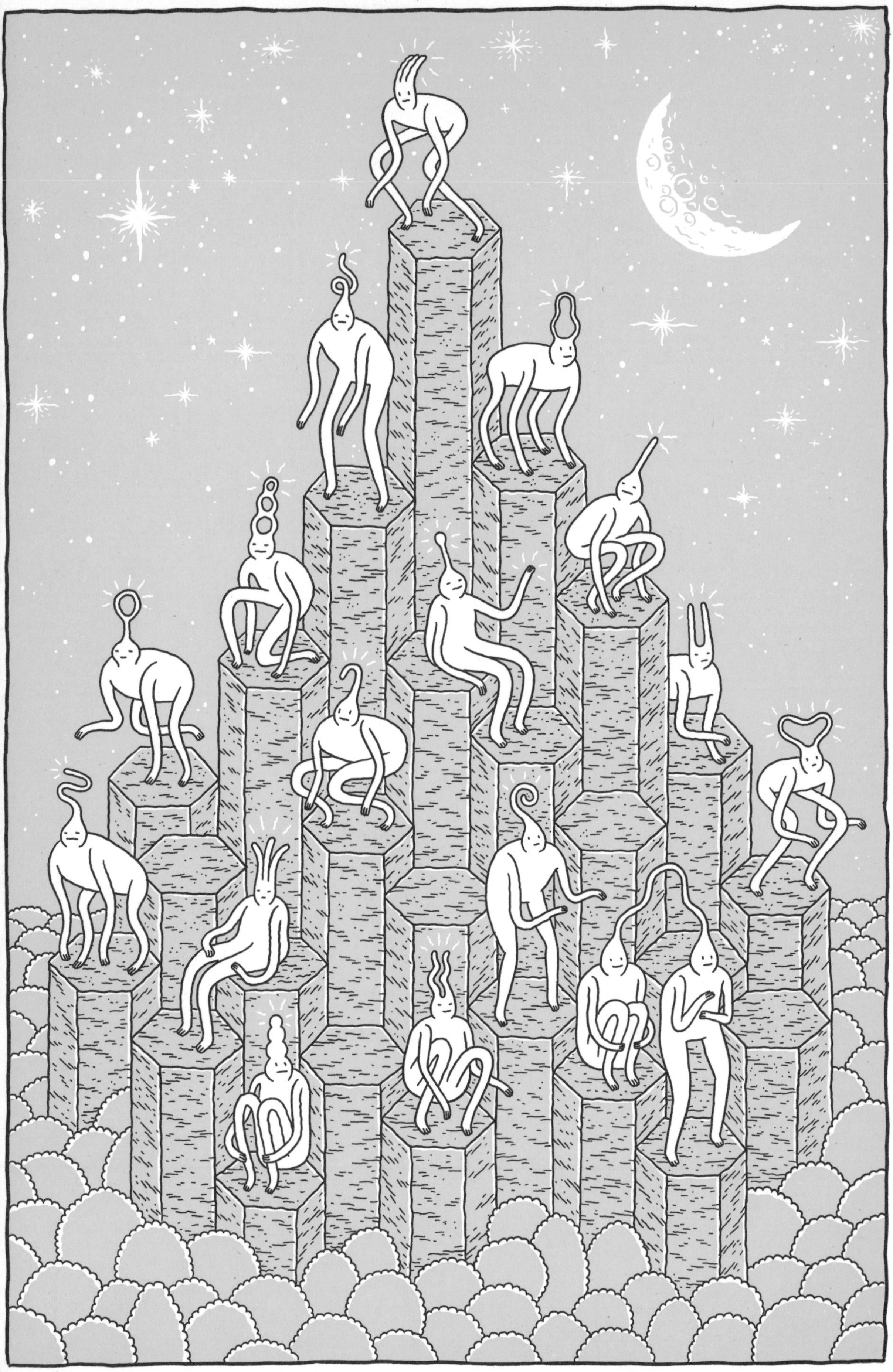

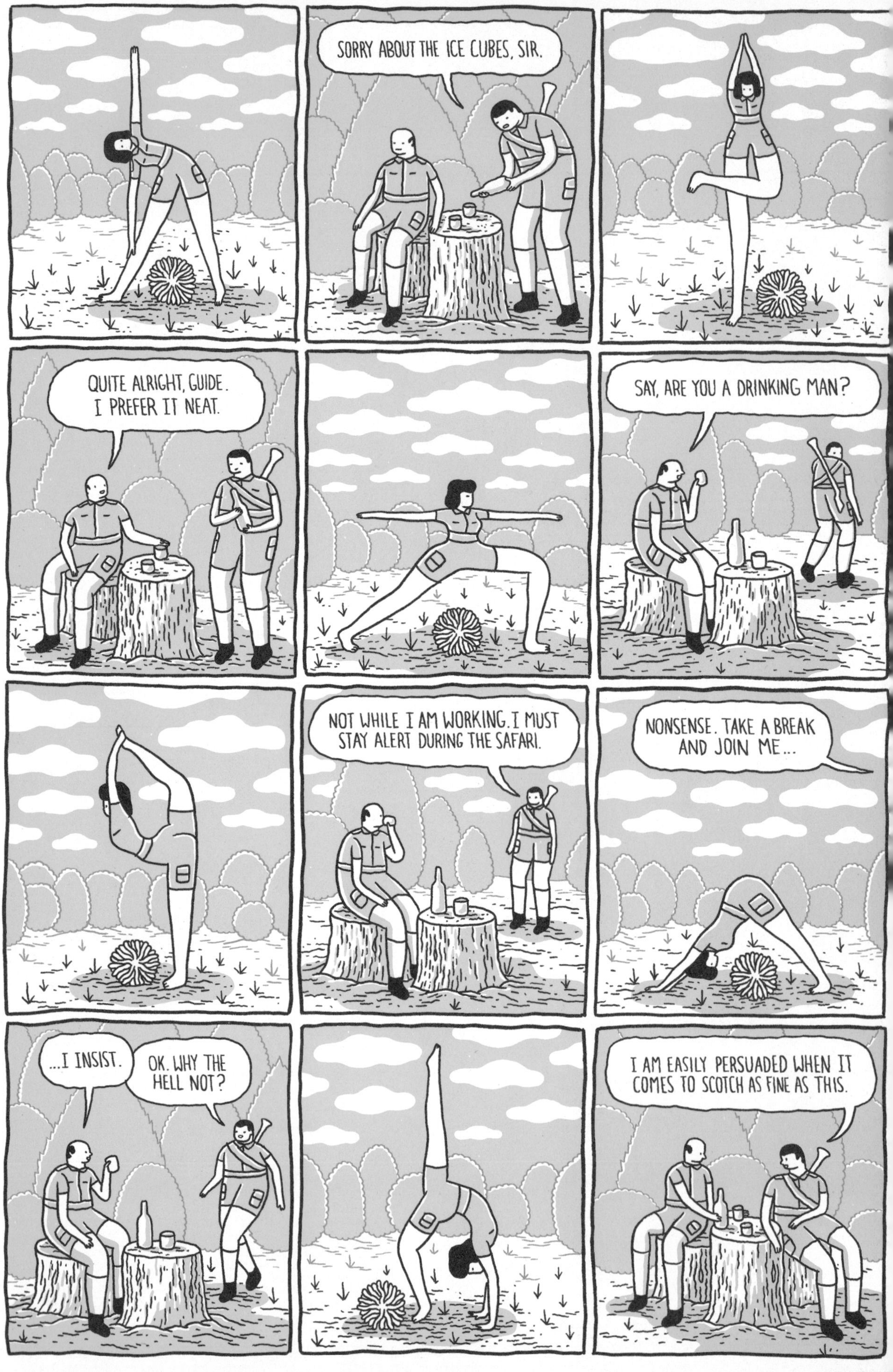
SORRY ABOUT THE ICE CUBES, SIR.
QUITE ALRIGHT, GUIDE. I PREFER IT NEAT.
SAY, ARE YOU A DRINKING MAN?
NOT WHILE I AM WORKING. I MUST STAY ALERT DURING THE SAFARI.
NONSENSE. TAKE A BREAK AND JOIN ME...
...I INSIST.
OK. WHY THE HELL NOT?
I AM EASILY PERSUADED WHEN IT COMES TO SCOTCH AS FINE AS THIS.

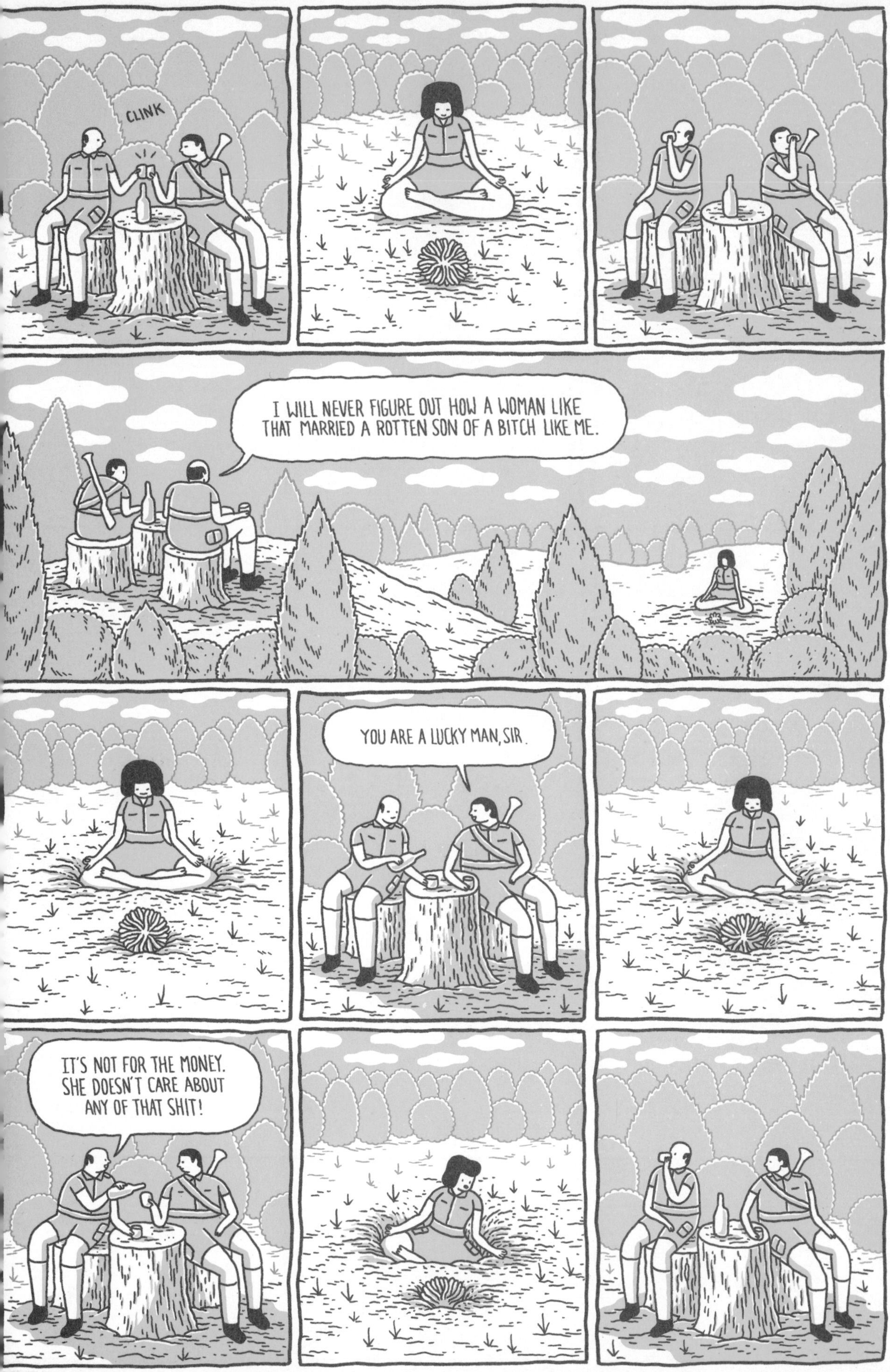
CLINK
I WILL NEVER FIGURE OUT HOW A WOMAN LIKE THAT MARRIED A ROTTEN SON OF A BITCH LIKE ME.
YOU ARE A LUCKY MAN, SIR.
IT'S NOT FOR THE MONEY. SHE DOESN'T CARE ABOUT ANY OF THAT SHIT!

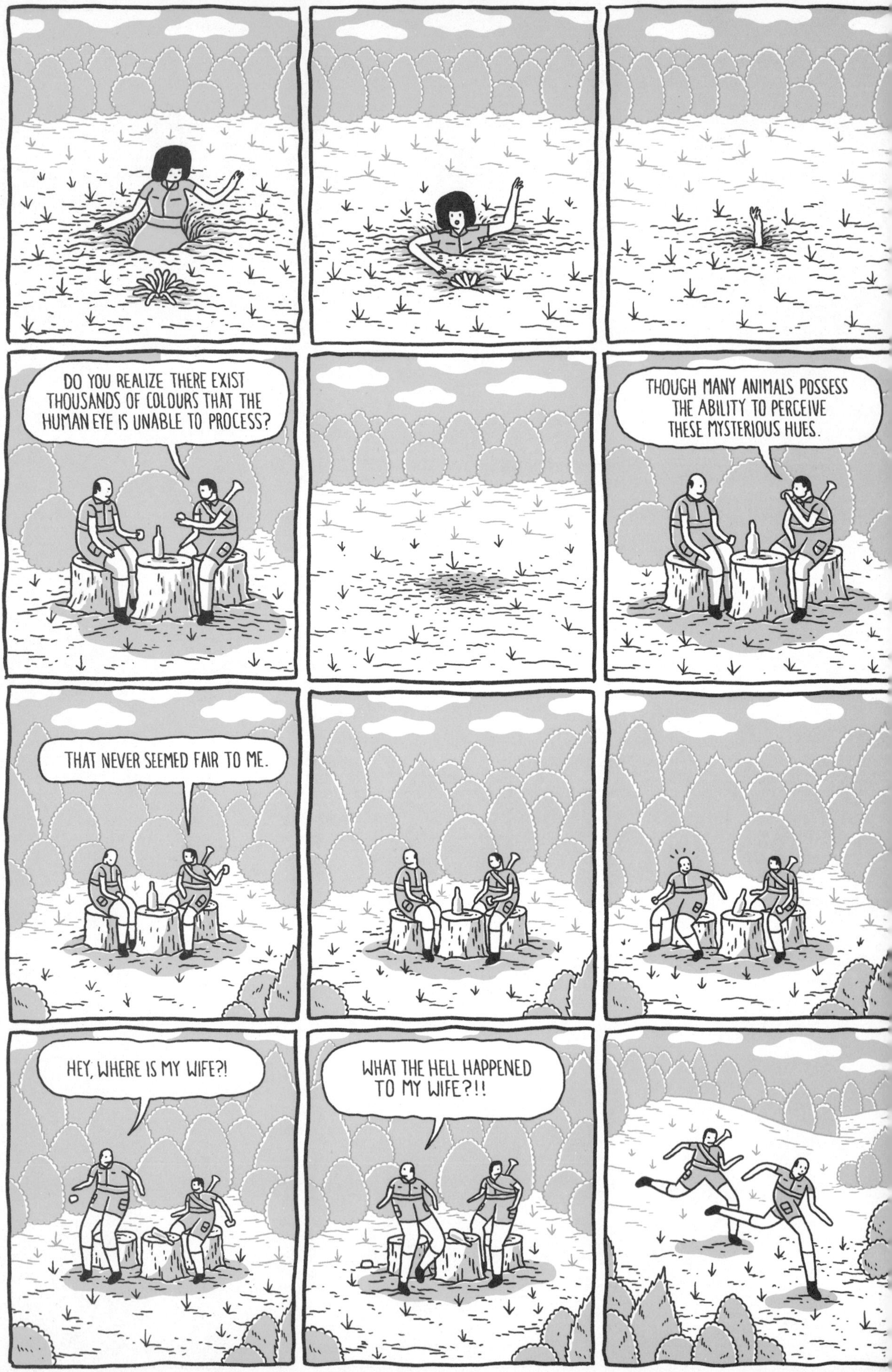
DO YOU REALIZE THERE EXIST THOUSANDS OF COLOURS THAT THE HUMAN EYE IS UNABLE TO PROCESS?
THOUGH MANY ANIMALS POSSESS THE ABILITY TO PERCEIVE THESE MYSTERIOUS HUES.
THAT NEVER SEEMED FAIR TO ME.
HEY, WHERE IS MY WIFE?!
WHAT THE HELL HAPPENED TO MY WIFE?!!

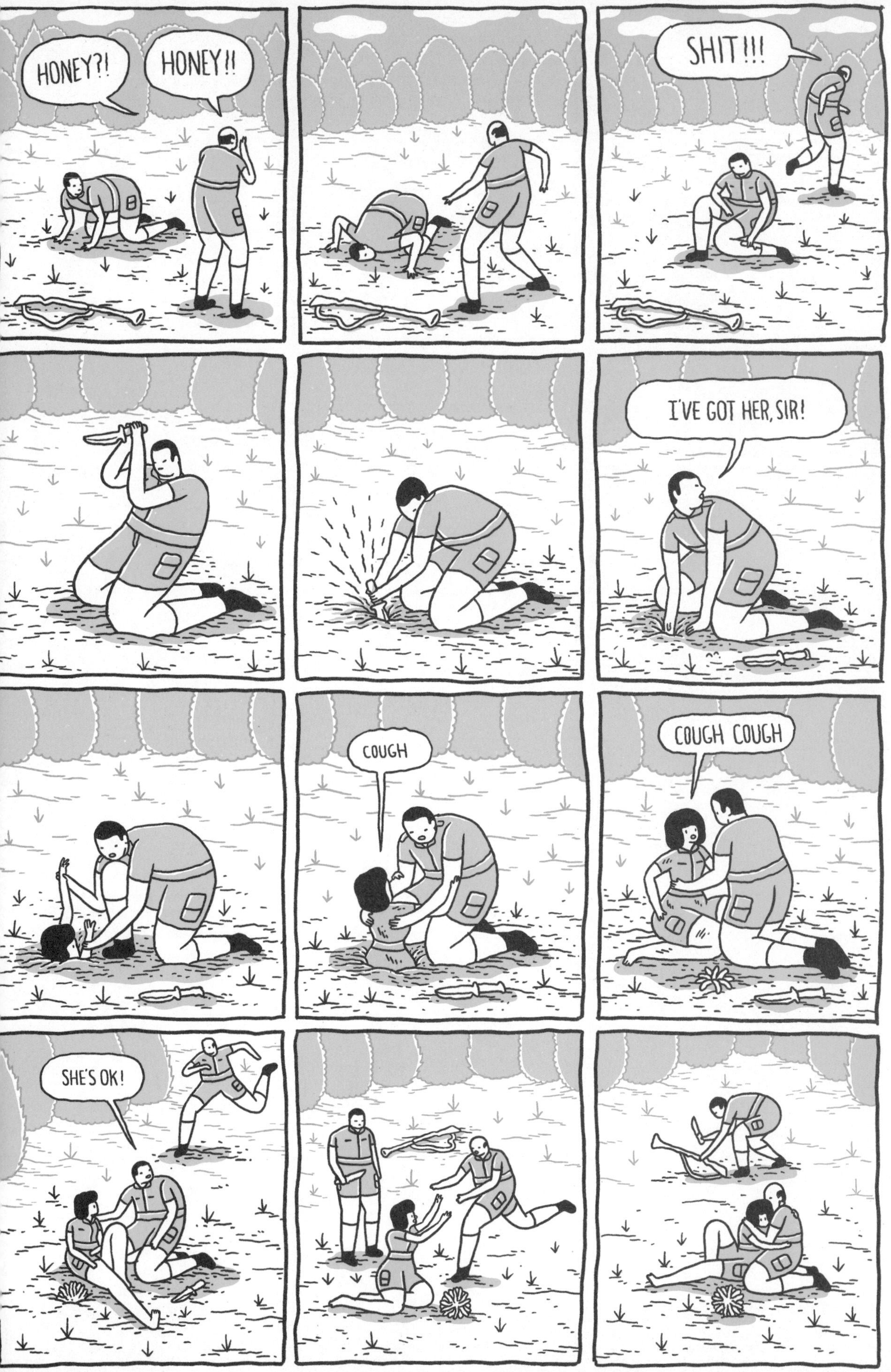
HONEY?!
HONEY!!
SHIT!!!
I'VE GOT HER, SIR!
COUGH
COUGH COUGH
SHE'S OK!

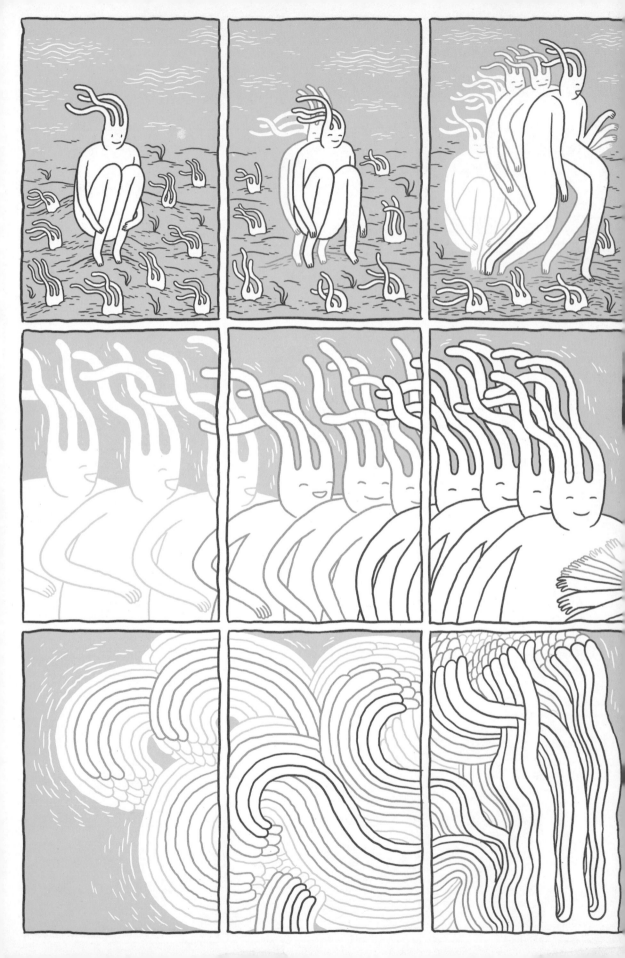

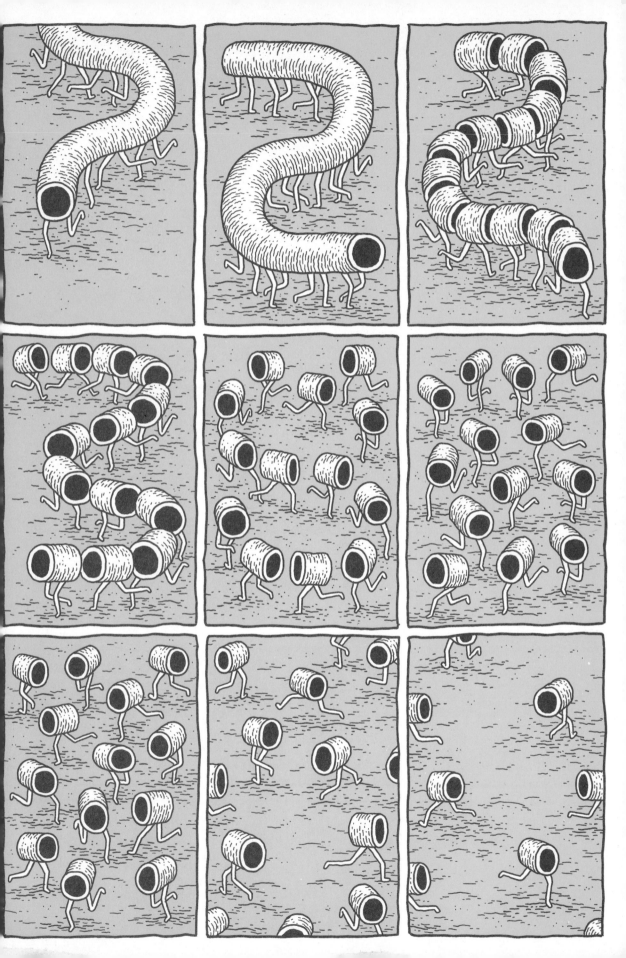

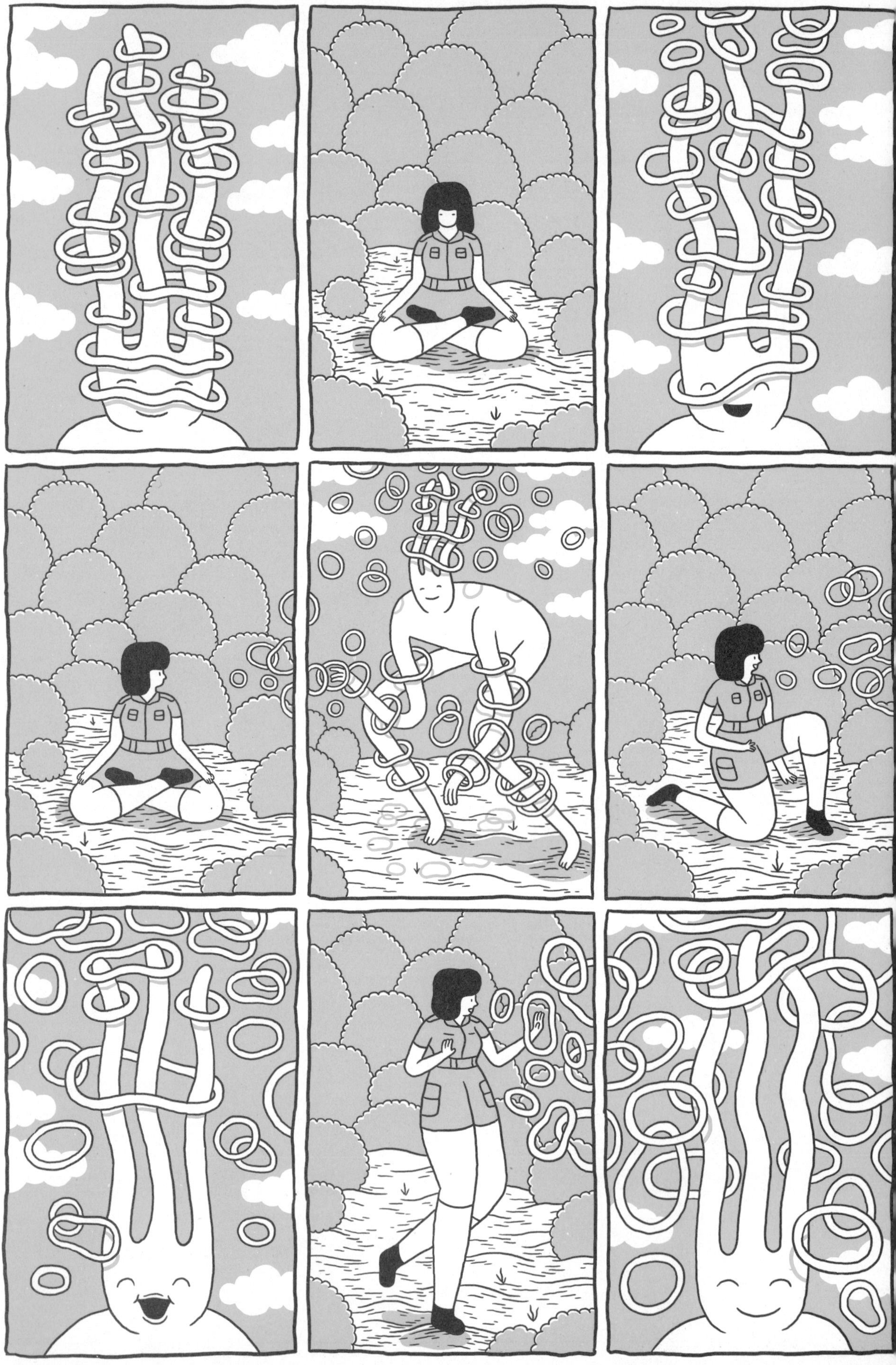

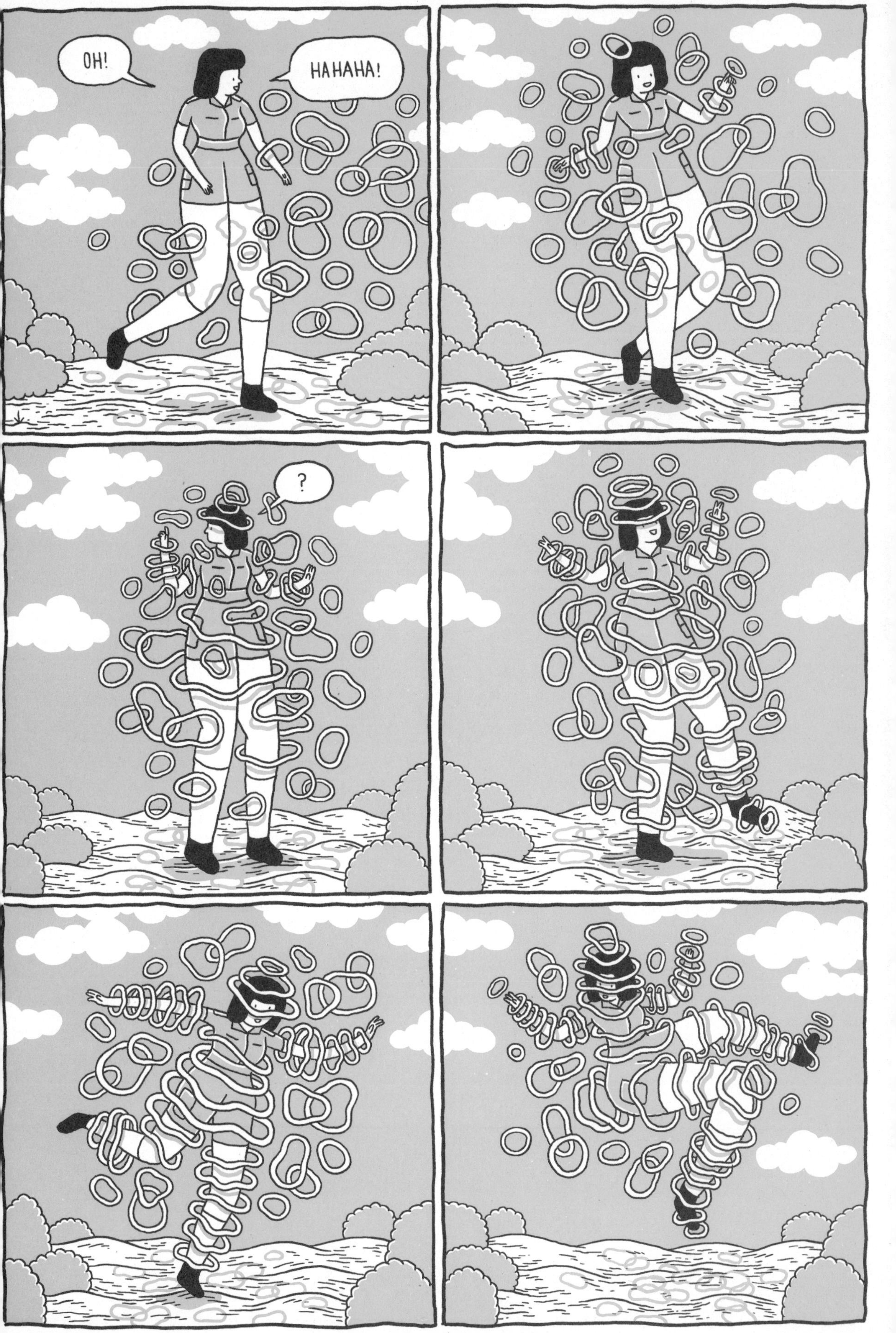
OH!
HAHAHA!
?

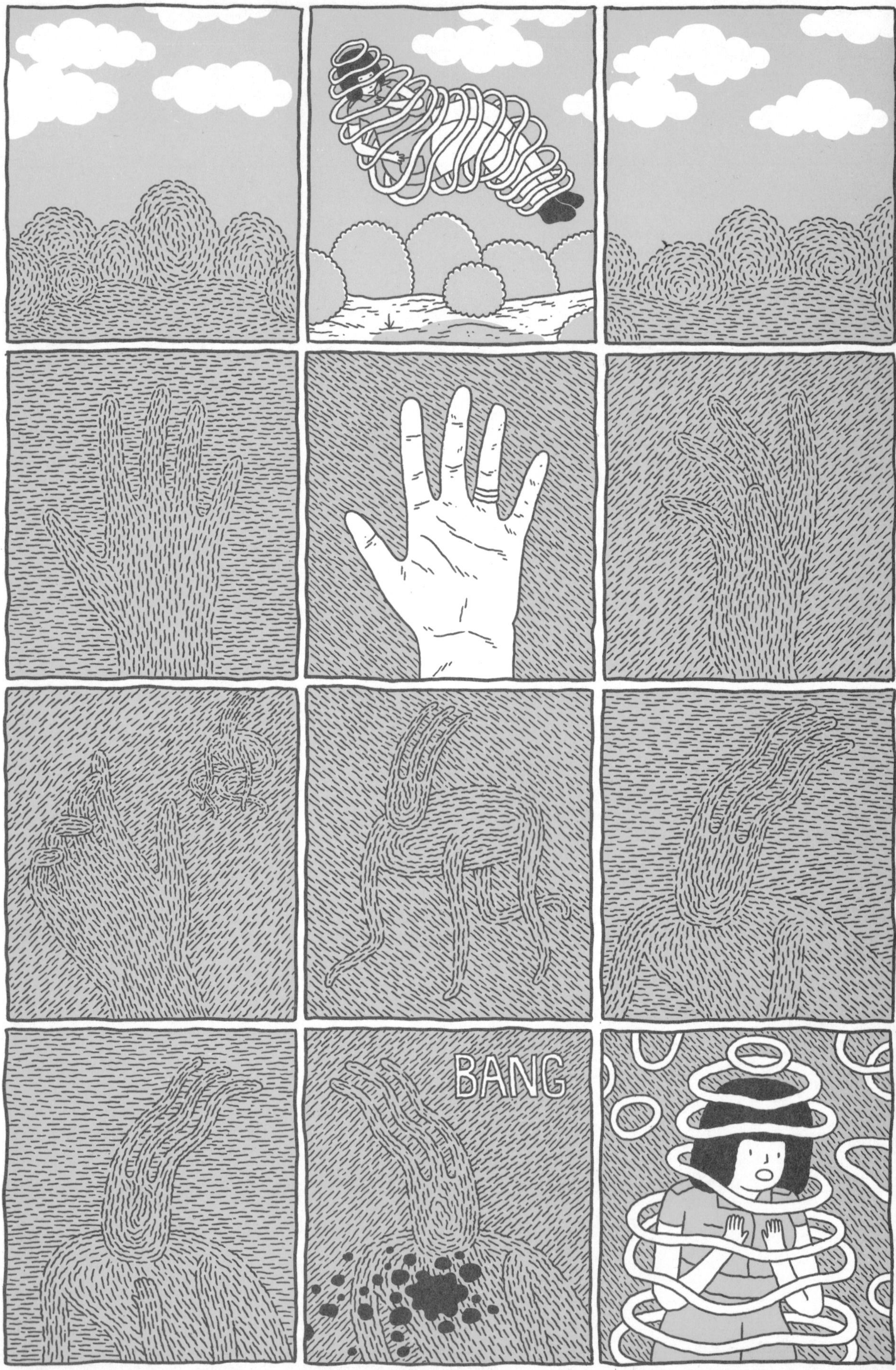
BANG

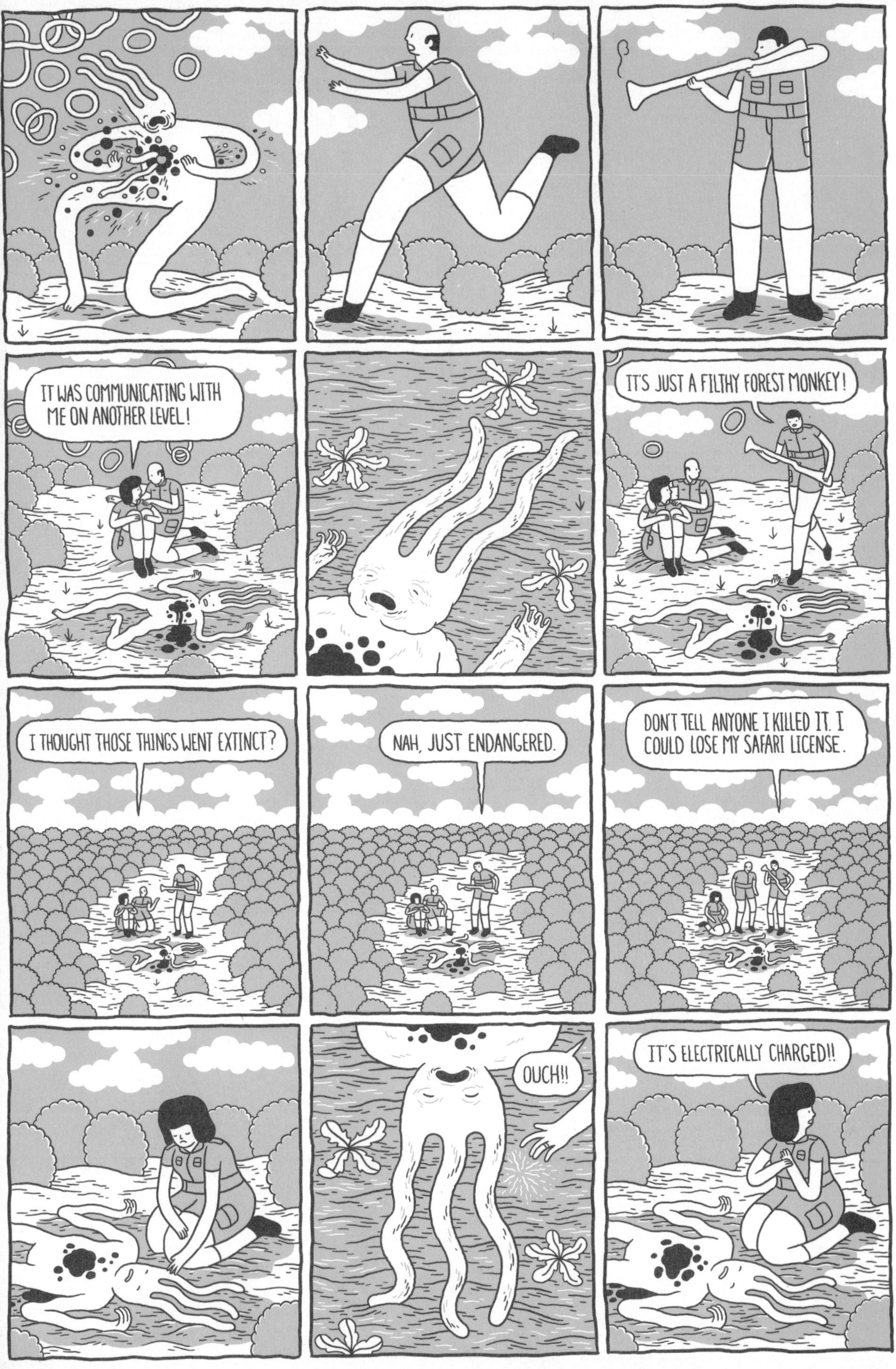

IT WAS COMMUNICATING WITH ME ON ANOTHER LEVEL!
IT'S JUST A FILTHY FOREST MONKEY!
I THOUGHT THOSE THINGS WENT EXTINCT?
NAH, JUST ENDANGERED.
DON'T TELL ANYONE I KILLED IT. I COULD LOSE MY SAFARI LICENSE.
OUCH!!
IT'S ELECTRICALLY CHARGED!!

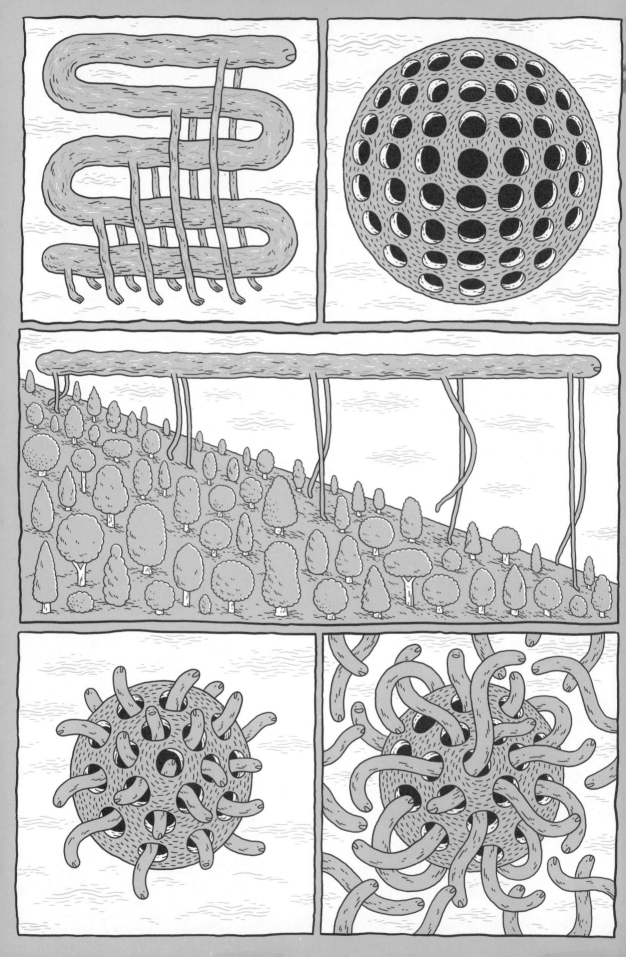

THE APPRENTICE IS REQUIRED TO MASTER MANY TECHNIQUES BEFORE RECEIVING SAFARI GUIDE CERTIFICATION.

AMONG THE MOST DIFFICULT AND ESSENTIAL OF THESE SKILLS IS THE ANCIENT PRACTICE OF UNIHEMISPHERIC SLOW-WAVE SLEEPING.

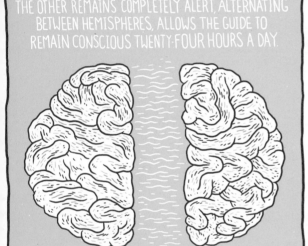

THE ABILITY TO SLEEP WITH HALF OF THE BRAIN WHILE THE OTHER REMAINS COMPLETELY ALERT, ALTERNATING BETWEEN HEMISPHERES, ALLOWS THE GUIDE TO REMAIN CONSCIOUS TWENTY-FOUR HOURS A DAY.

THIS UNCONVENTIONAL METHOD HAS BEEN OBSERVED IN A NUMBER OF TERRESTRIAL, AQUATIC AND AVIAN SPECIES, PARTICULARLY THOSE THAT DWELL IN AREAS OF HIGH PREDATION.

IT IS STRONGLY RECOMMENDED THAT SAFARI GUIDES AVOID FULL REM SLEEP WHILE GUIDING SAFARIS.

THOUGH, WHEN CHARGED WITH THE CARE OF THE MOST DEMANDING AND PAMPERED OF CLIENTS, A TRADITIONAL FIFTEEN-MINUTE NAP IS OCCASIONALLY PERMITTED.

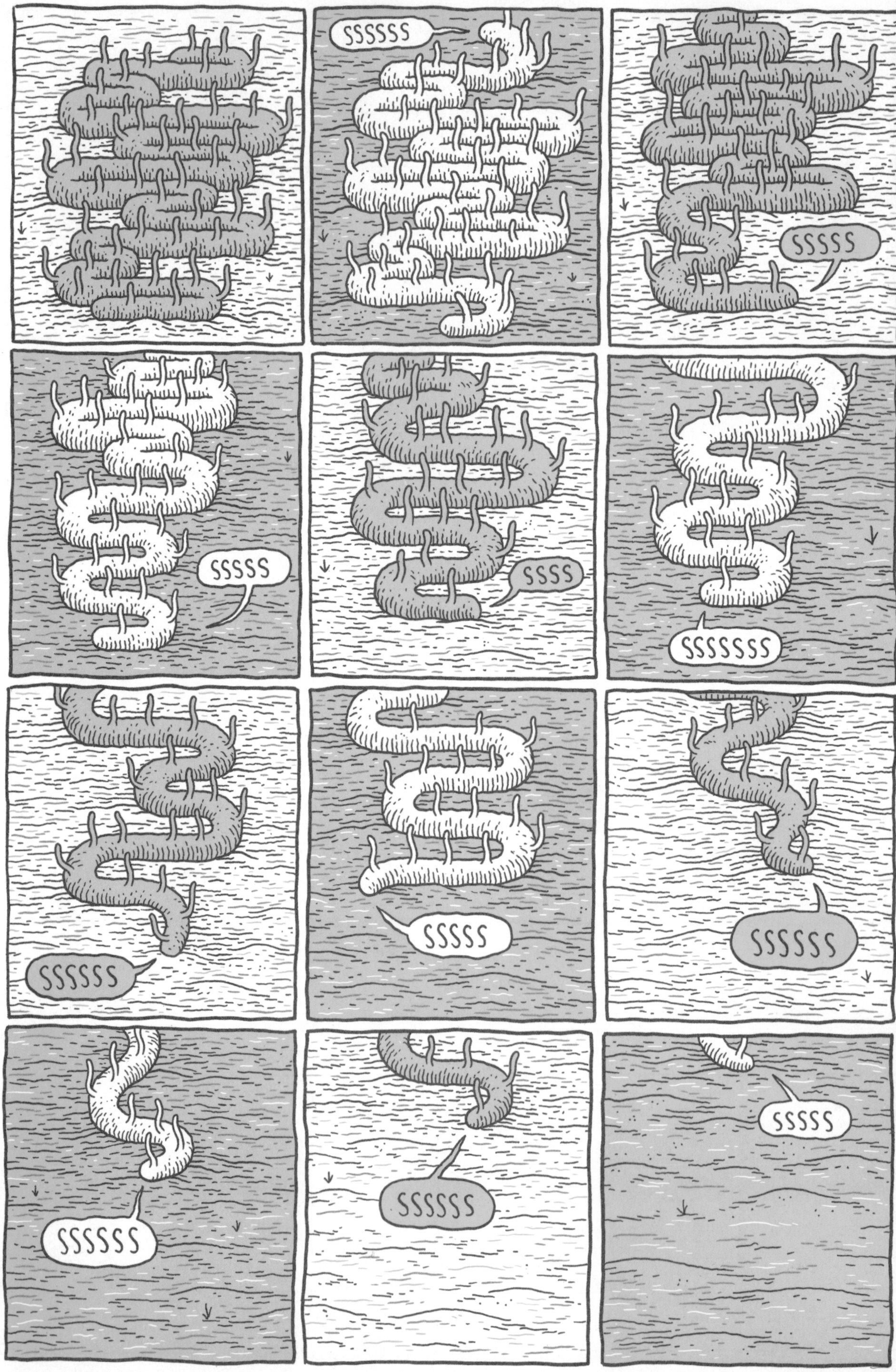
SSSSSS
SSSSS
SSSSS
SSSS
SSSSSSS
SSSSSS
SSSSS
SSSSSS
SSSSSS
SSSSSS
SSSSS

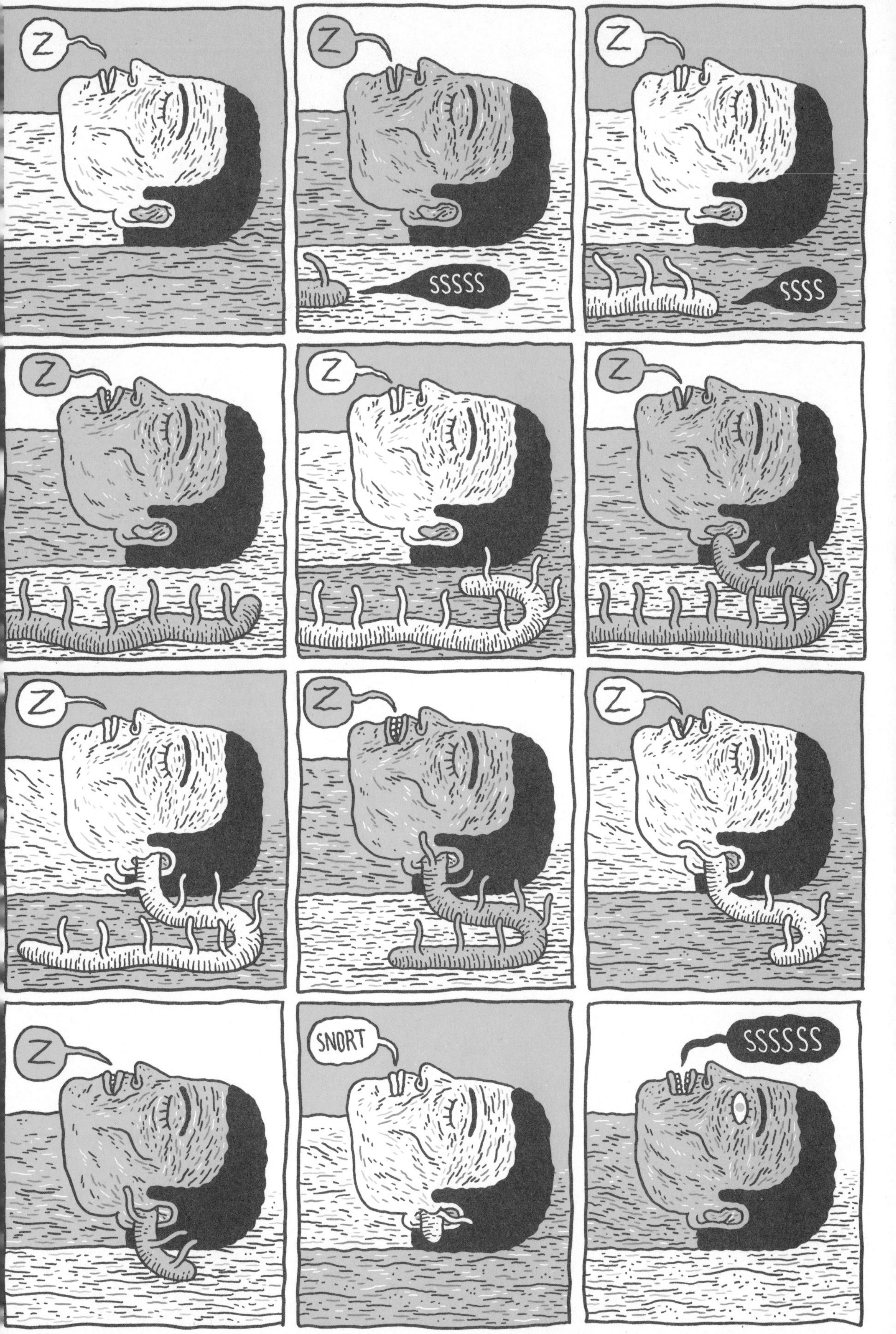
Z
Z
SSSSS
Z
SSSS
Z
Z
Z
Z
Z
Z
Z
SNORT
SSSSSS

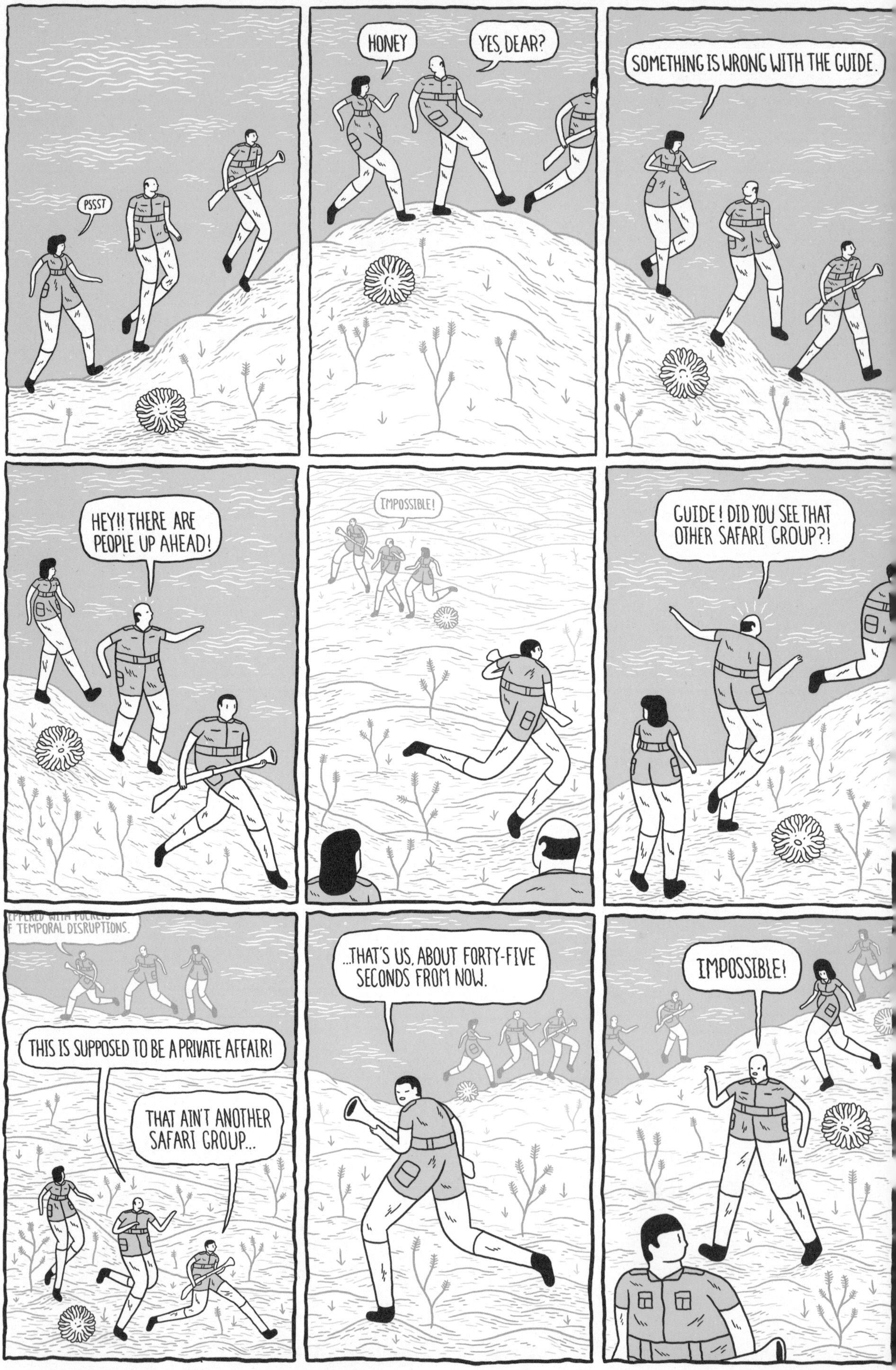
PSSST
HONEY
YES, DEAR?
SOMETHING IS WRONG WITH THE GUIDE.
HEY!! THERE ARE PEOPLE UP AHEAD!
IMPOSSIBLE!
GUIDE! DID YOU SEE THAT OTHER SAFARI GROUP?!
F TEMPORAL DISRUPTIONS.
THIS IS SUPPOSED TO BE A PRIVATE AFFAIR!
THAT AIN'T ANOTHER SAFARI GROUP...
...THAT'S US, ABOUT FORTY-FIVE SECONDS FROM NOW.
IMPOSSIBLE!

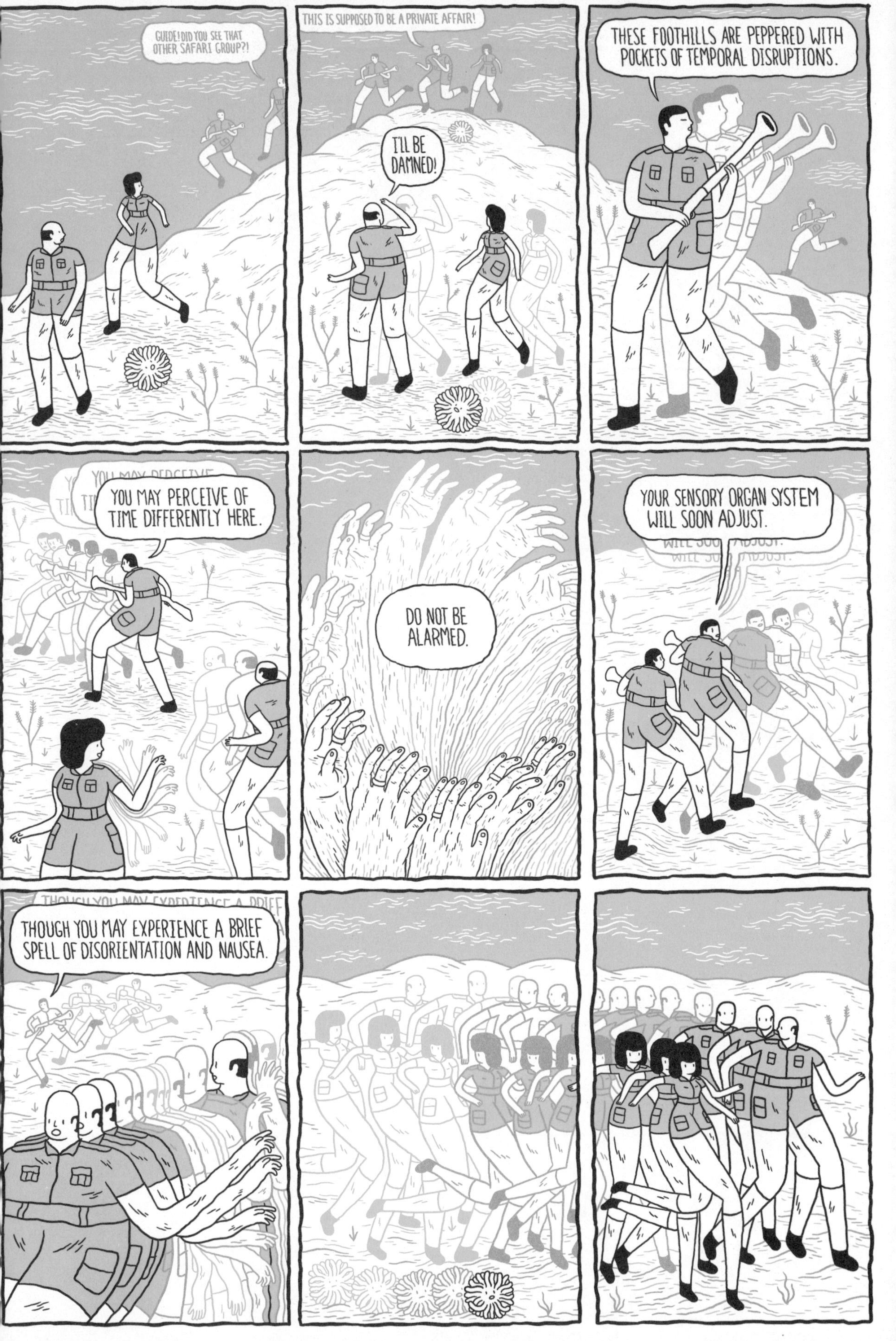
GUIDE! DID YOU SEE THAT OTHER SAFARI GROUP?!
THIS IS SUPPOSED TO BE A PRIVATE AFFAIR!
I'LL BE DAMNED!
THESE FOOTHILLS ARE PEPPERED WITH POCKETS OF TEMPORAL DISRUPTIONS.
YOU MAY PERCEIVE OF TIME DIFFERENTLY HERE.
DO NOT BE ALARMED.
YOUR SENSORY ORGAN SYSTEM WILL SOON ADJUST.
THOUGH YOU MAY EXPERIENCE A BRIEF SPELL OF DISORIENTATION AND NAUSEA.

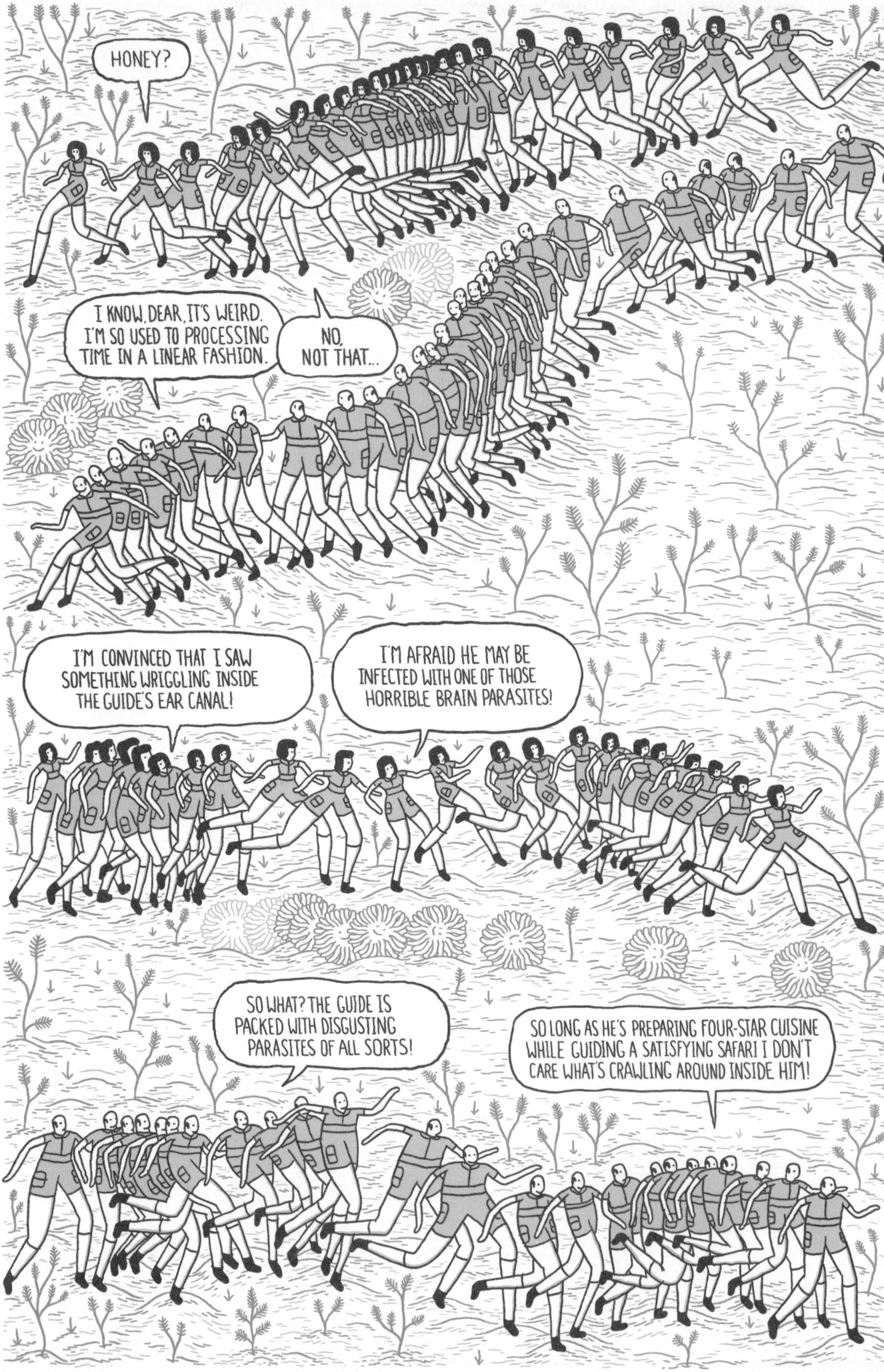
HONEY?
I KNOW, DEAR, IT'S WEIRD. I'M SO USED TO PROCESSING TIME IN A LINEAR FASHION.
NO, NOT THAT...
I'M CONVINCED THAT I SAW SOMETHING WRIGGLING INSIDE THE GUIDE'S EAR CANAL!
I'M AFRAID HE MAY BE INFECTED WITH ONE OF THOSE HORRIBLE BRAIN PARASITES!
SO WHAT? THE GUIDE IS PACKED WITH DISGUSTING PARASITES OF ALL SORTS!
SO LONG AS HE'S PREPARING FOUR-STAR CUISINE WHILE GUIDING A SATISFYING SAFARI I DON'T CARE WHAT'S CRAWLING AROUND INSIDE HIM!

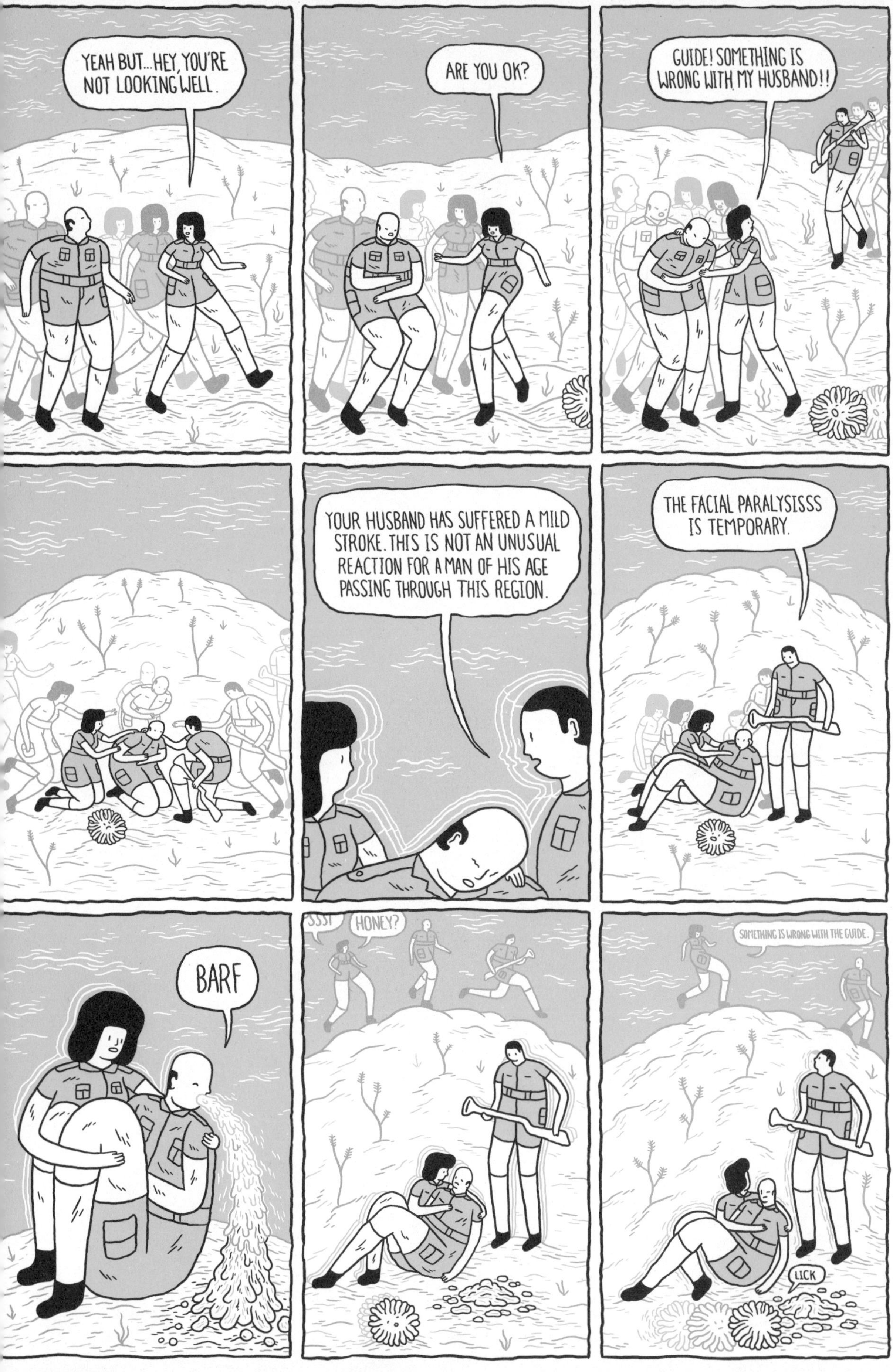
YEAH BUT... HEY, YOU'RE NOT LOOKING WELL.
ARE YOU OK?
GUIDE! SOMETHING IS WRONG WITH MY HUSBAND!!
YOUR HUSBAND HAS SUFFERED A MILD STROKE. THIS IS NOT AN UNUSUAL REACTION FOR A MAN OF HIS AGE PASSING THROUGH THIS REGION.
THE FACIAL PARALYSISSS IS TEMPORARY.
BARF
HONEY?
SOMETHING IS WRONG WITH THE GUIDE.
LICK

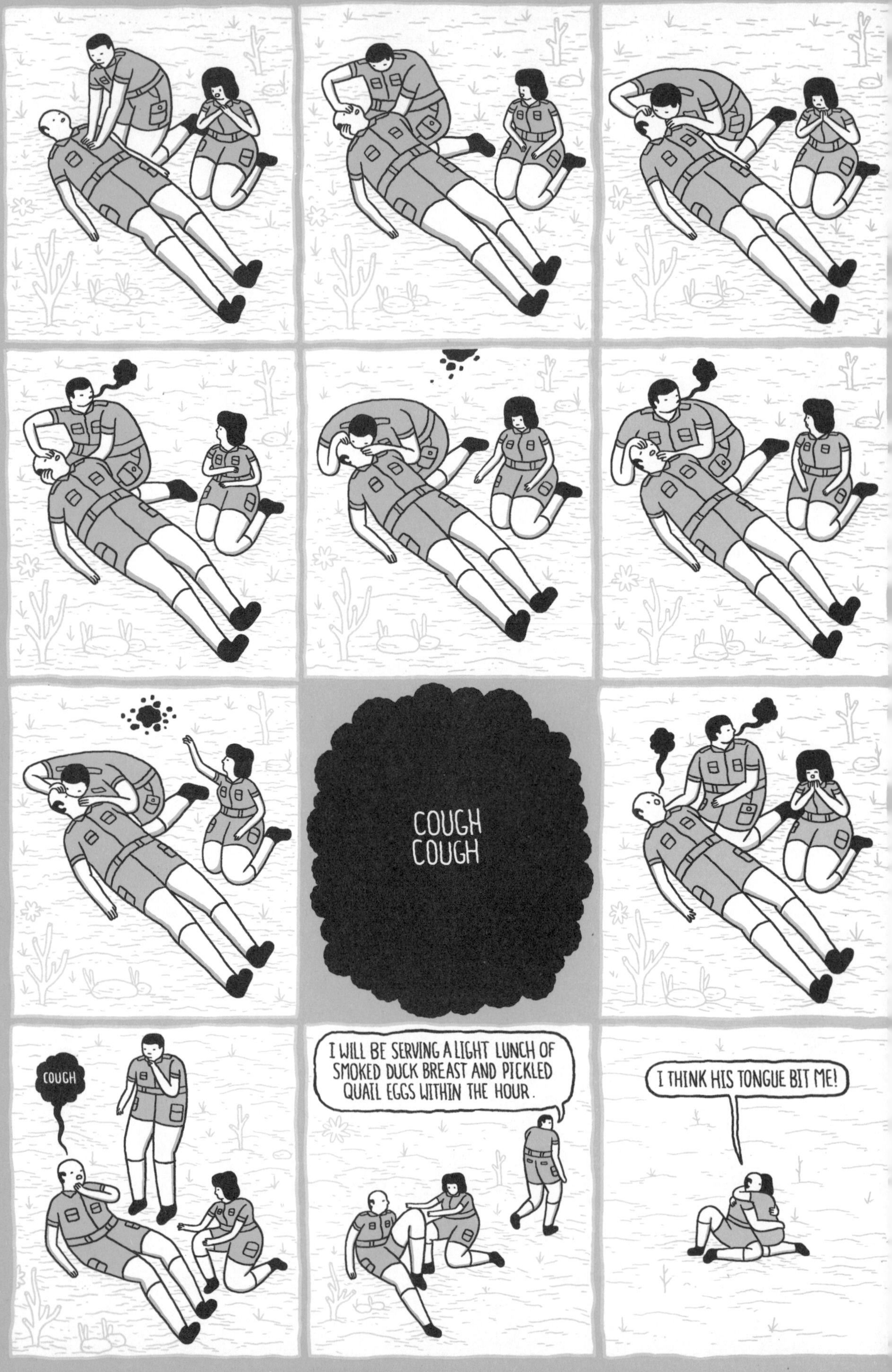
COUGH
COUGH
COUGH
I WILL BE SERVING A LIGHT LUNCH OF SMOKED DUCK BREAST AND PICKLED QUAIL EGGS WITHIN THE HOUR.
I THINK HIS TONGUE BIT ME!

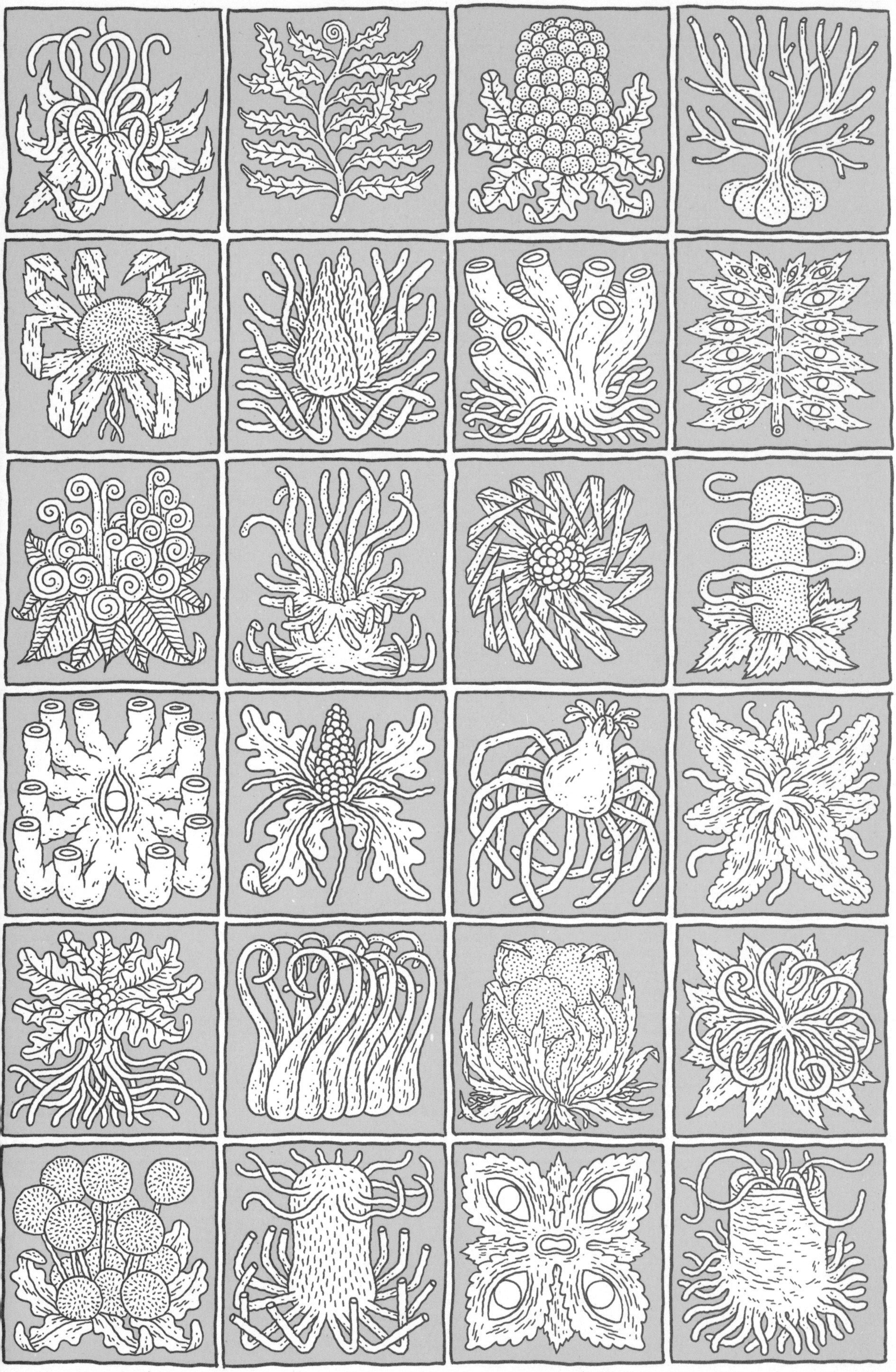

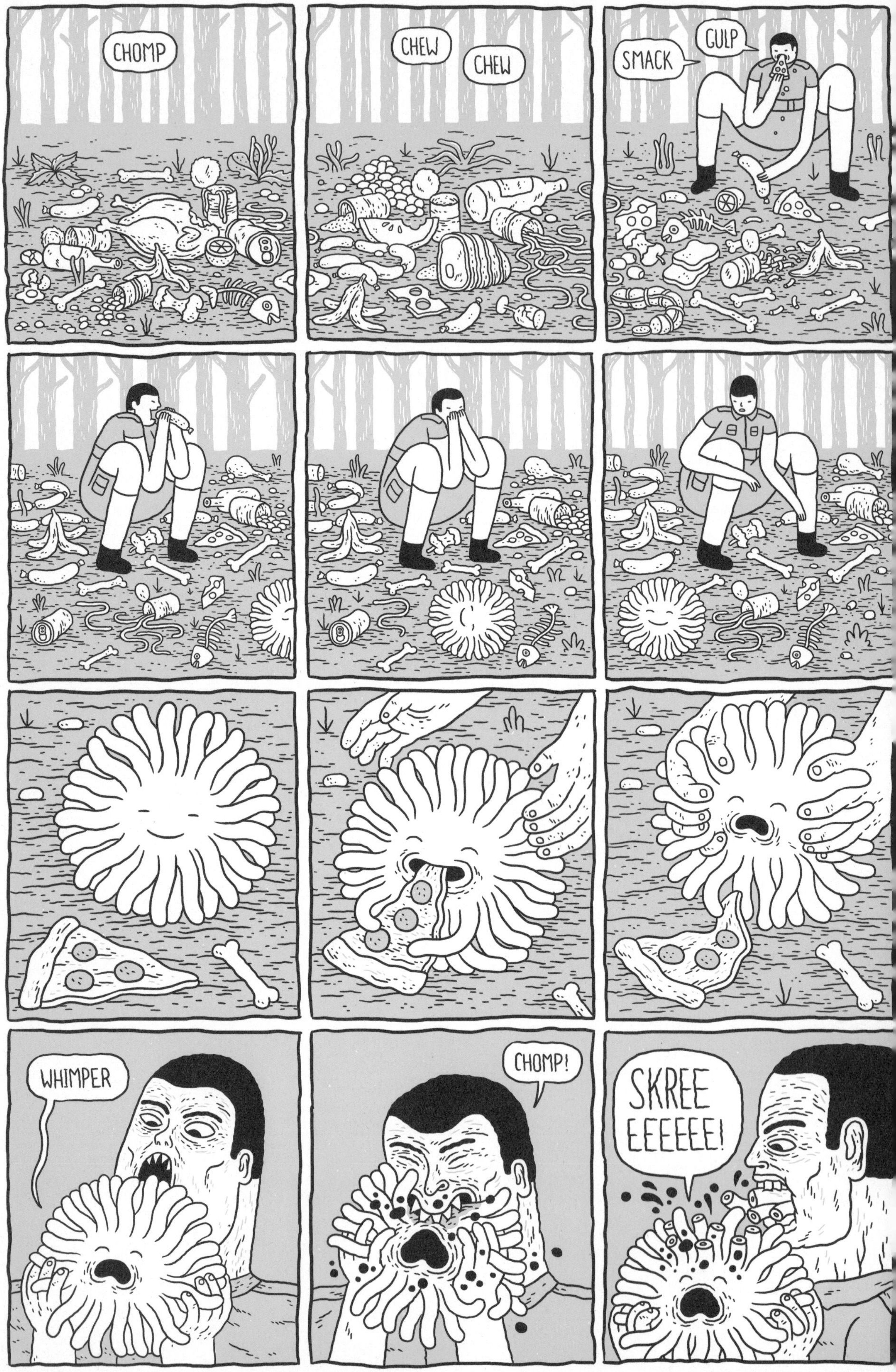
CHOMP
CHEW
CHEW
SMACK
GULP
WHIMPER
CHOMP!
SKREE
EEEEEE!

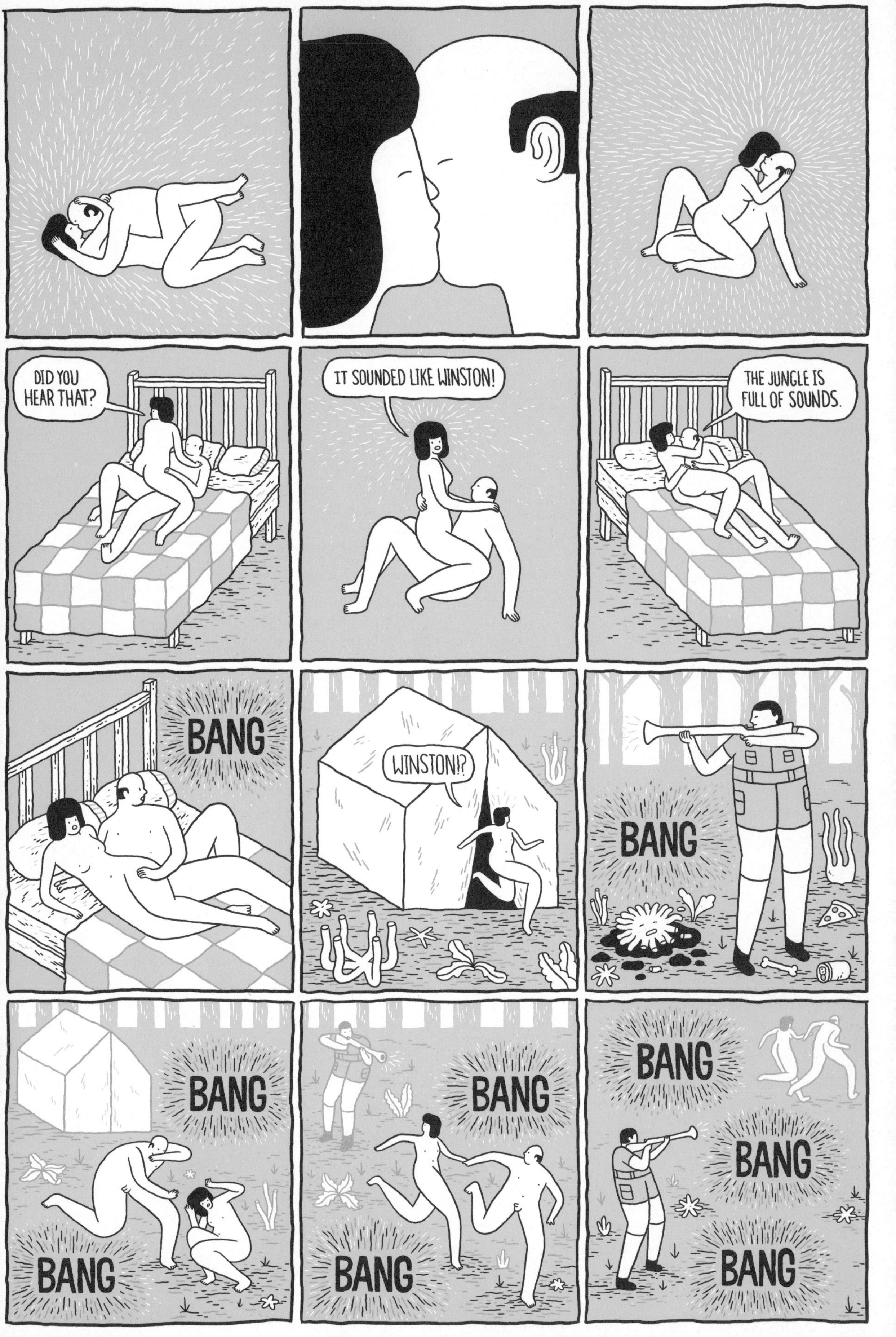
DID YOU HEAR THAT?
IT SOUNDED LIKE WINSTON!
THE JUNGLE IS FULL OF SOUNDS.
BANG
WINSTON!?
BANG
BANG
BANG
BANG
BANG
BANG
BANG
BANG

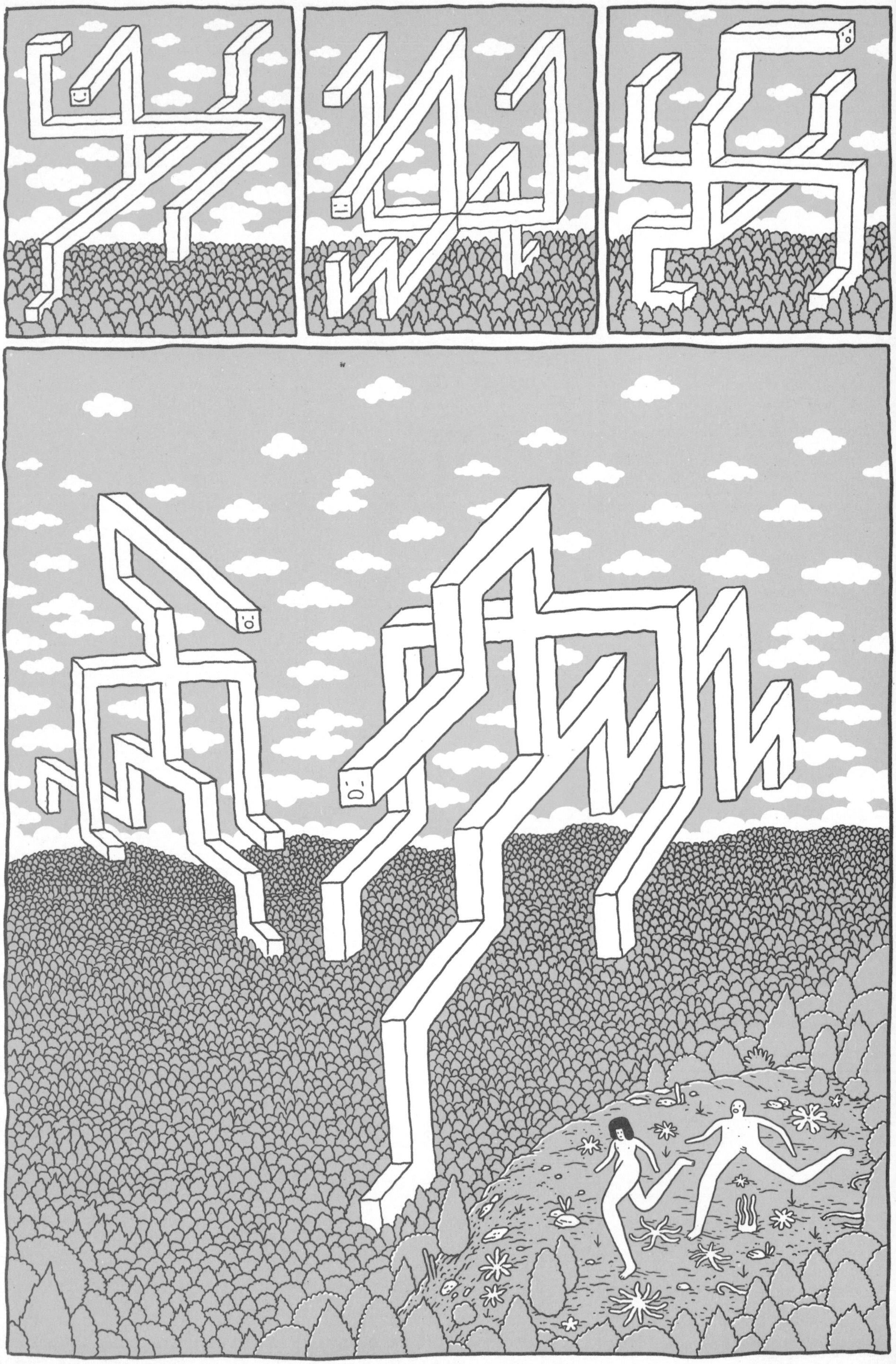

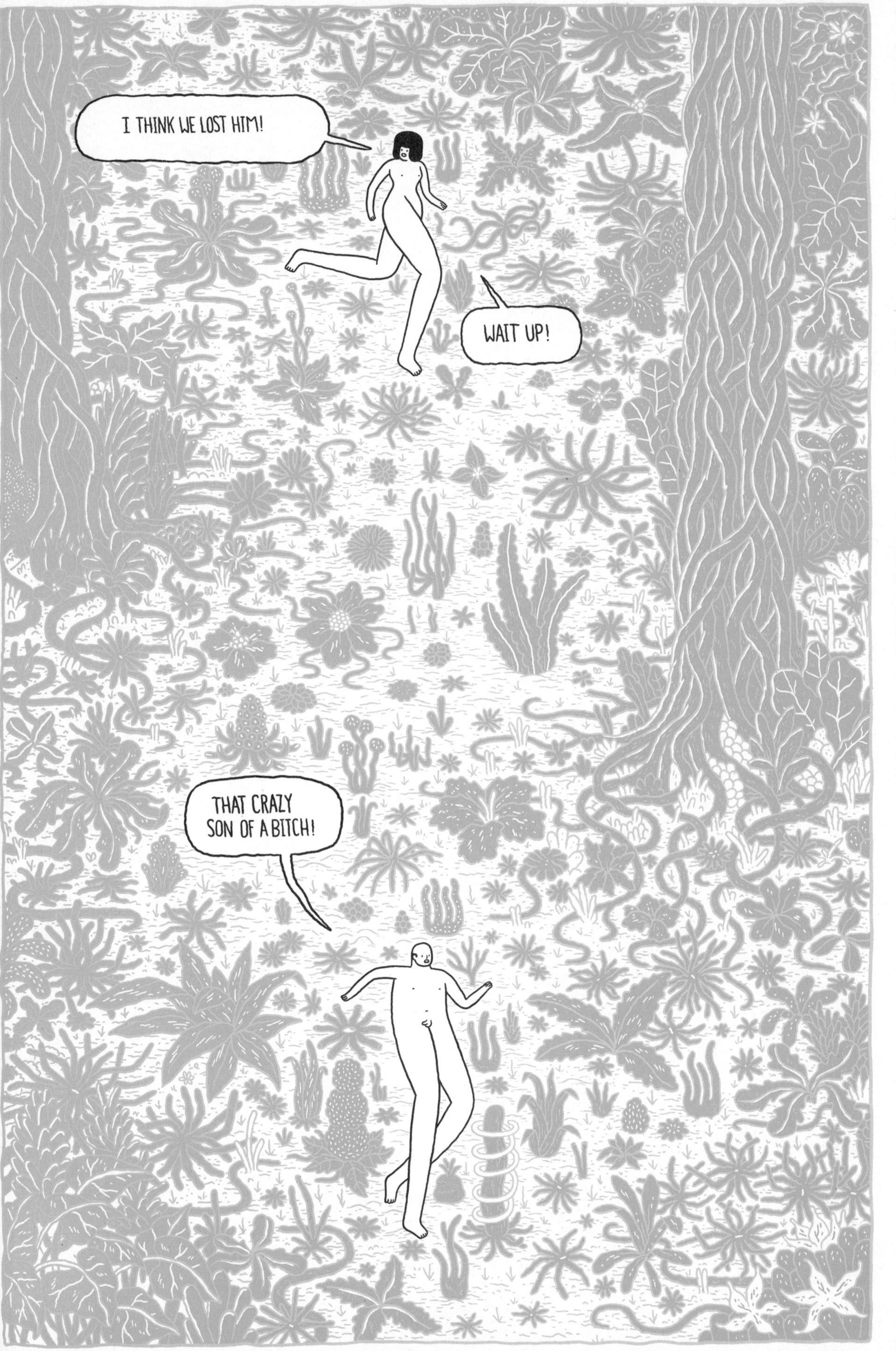
I THINK WE LOST HIM!
WAIT UP!
THAT CRAZY SON OF A BITCH!

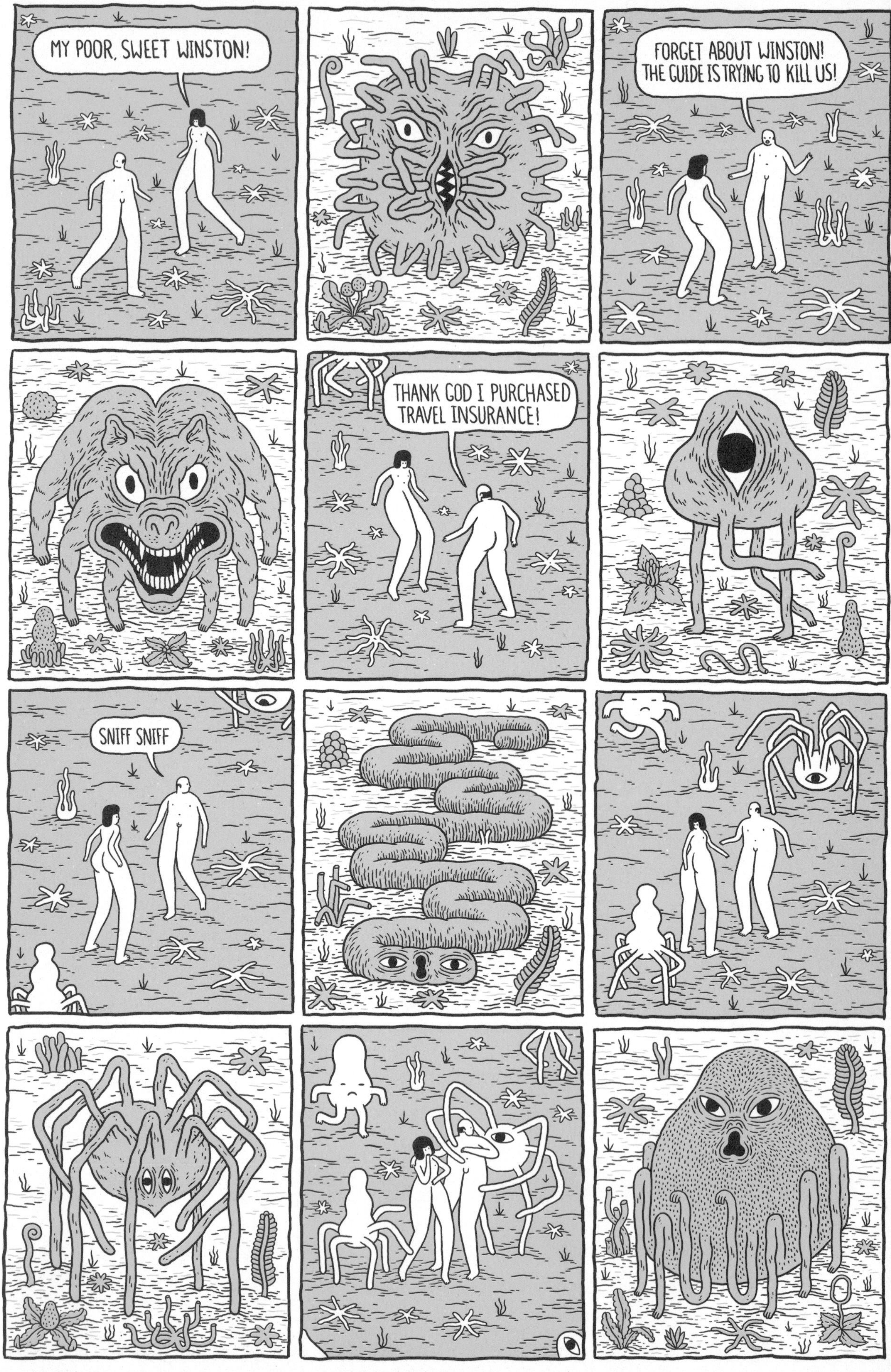
MY POOR, SWEET WINSTON!
FORGET ABOUT WINSTON! THE GUIDE IS TRYING TO KILL US!
THANK GOD I PURCHASED TRAVEL INSURANCE!
SNIFF SNIFF

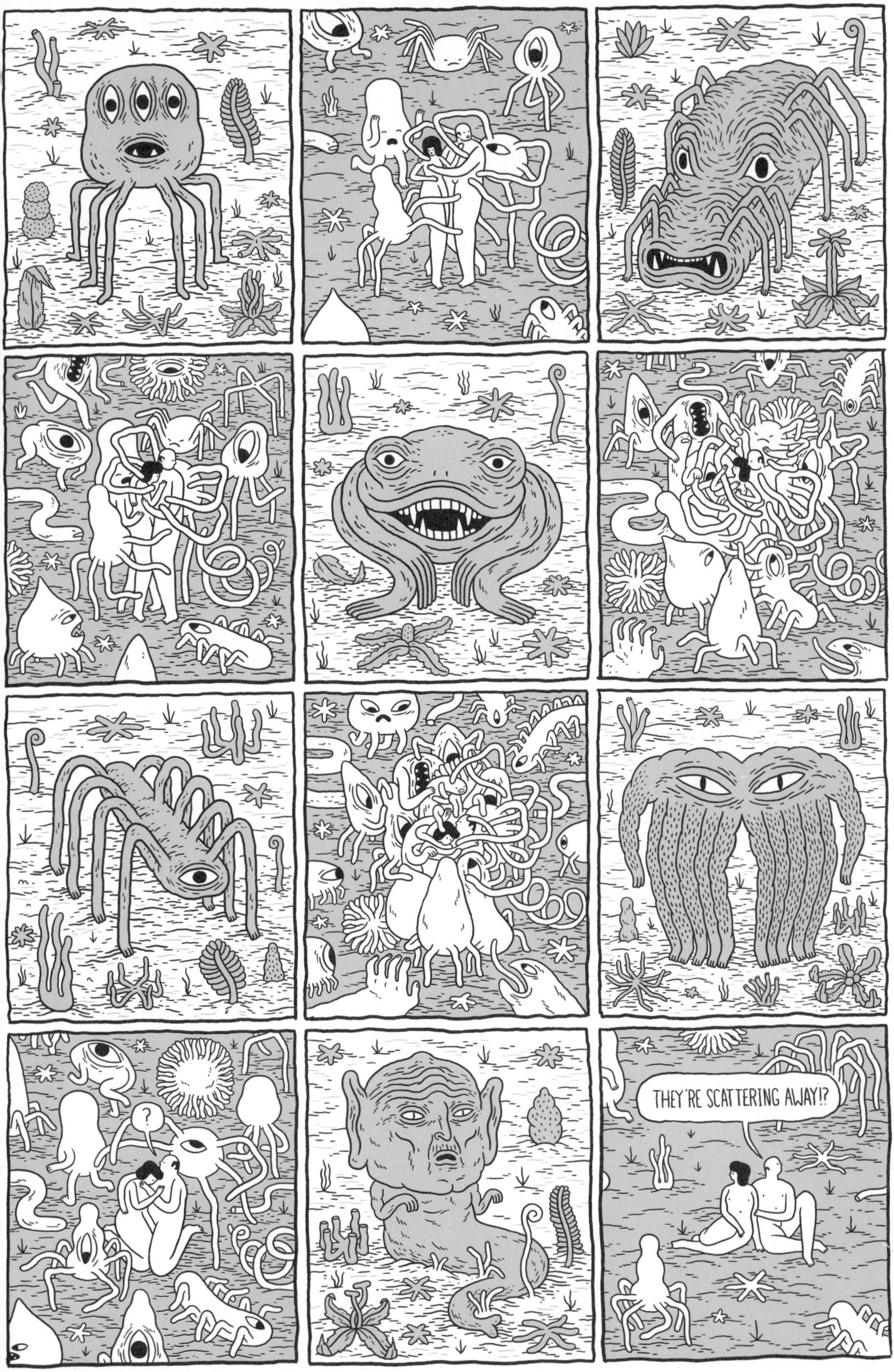
THEY'RE SCATTERING AWAY!?

SOMETHING MUST HAVE SPOOKED THEM!

LOOK!

SHIT!

IT'S THOSE DAMN MONKEYS AGAIN!

I THINK THEY WANT TO HELP US... CAREFUL, DEAR!

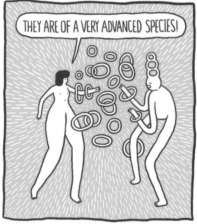

THEY ARE OF A VERY ADVANCED SPECIES!

THEY USE THEIR ANTENNAE TO COMMUNICATE.

BANG

BANG

BANG

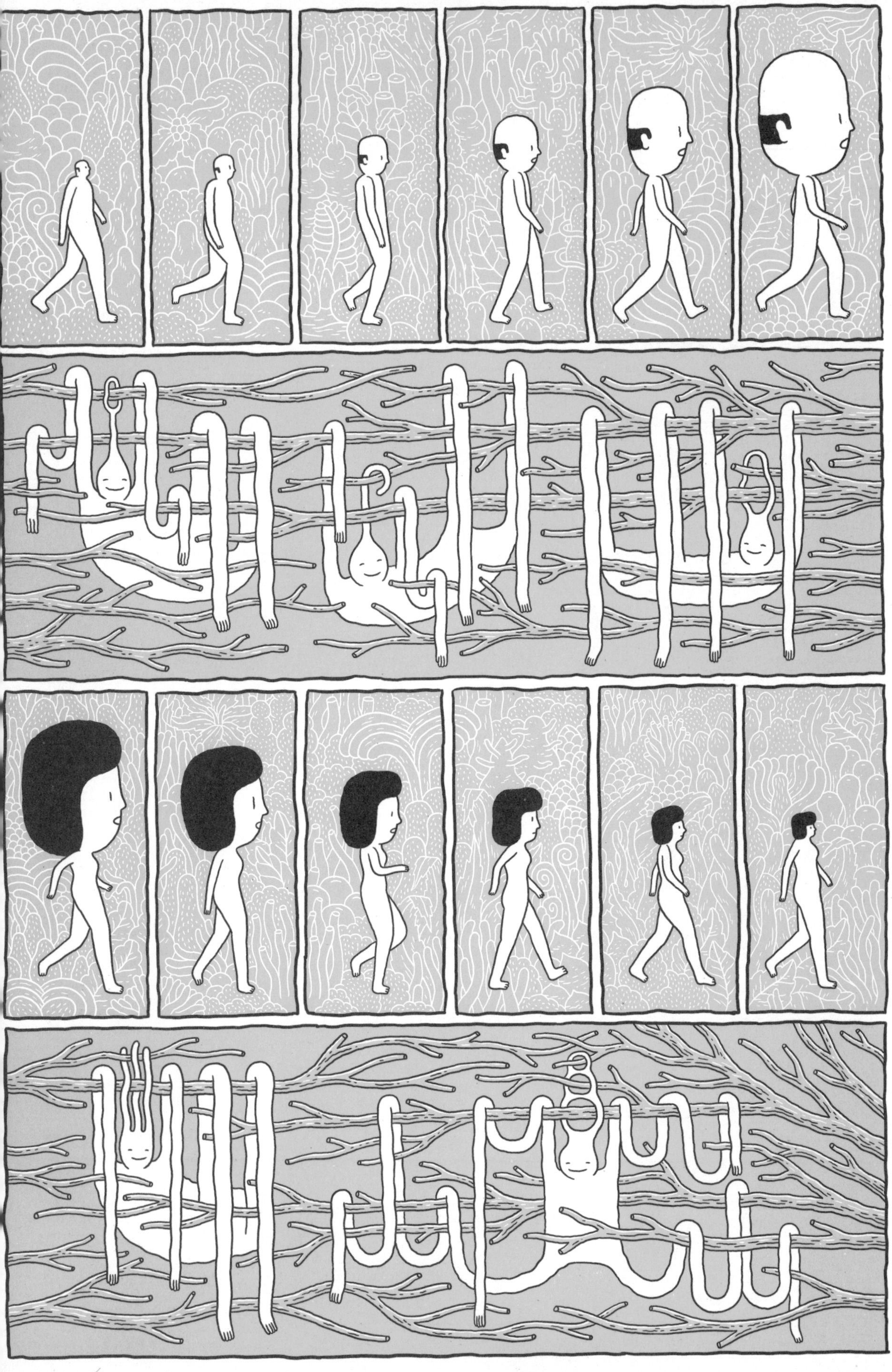

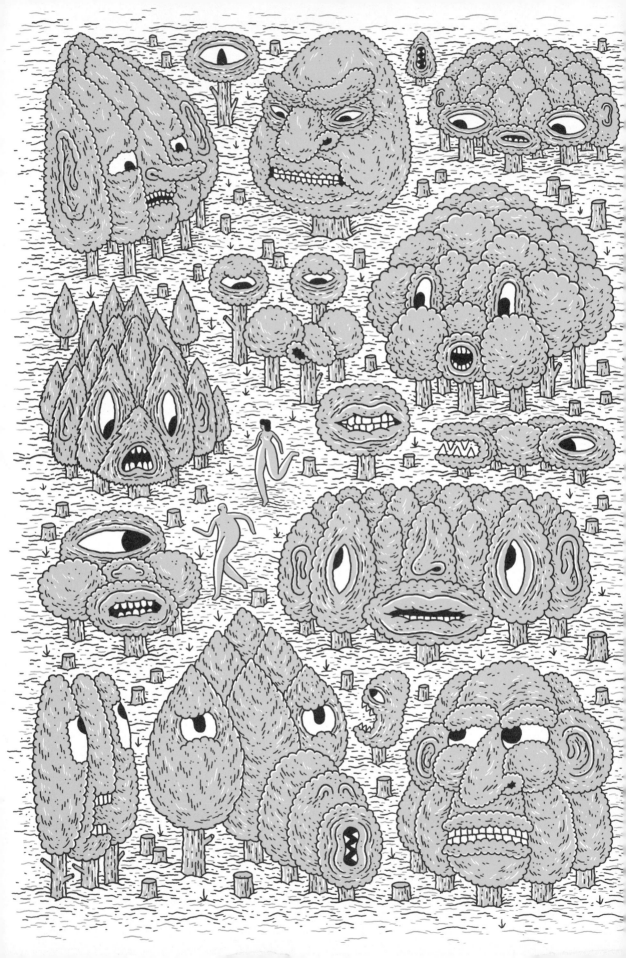

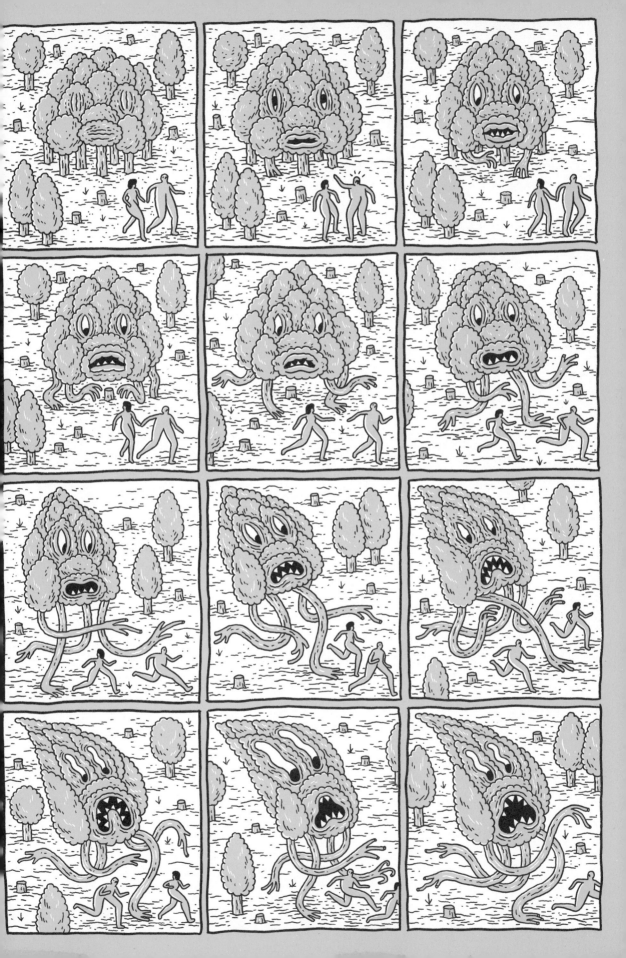

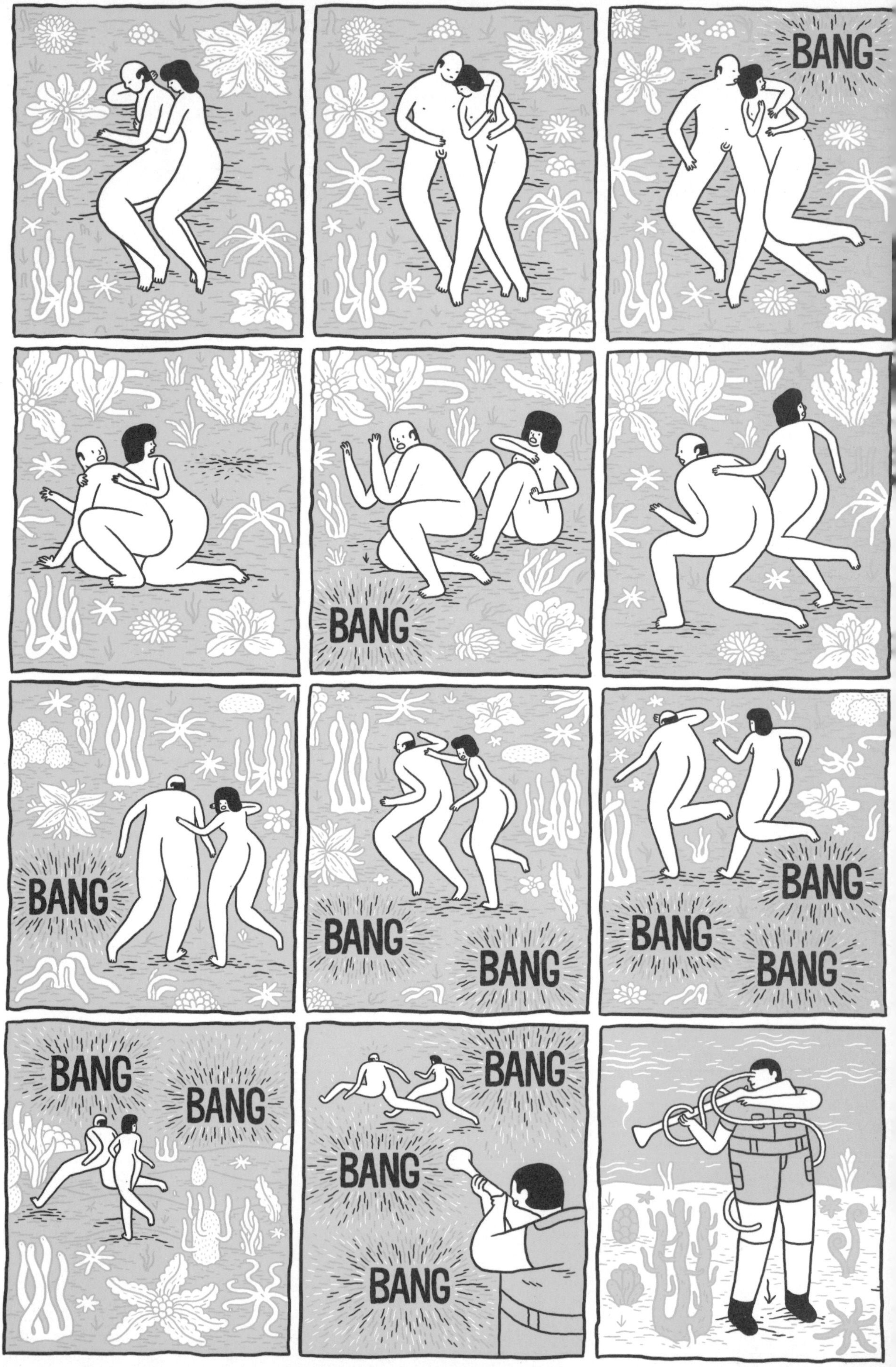
BANG
BANG
BANG
BANG
BANG
BANG
BANG
BANG
BANG
BANG
BANG
BANG
BANG
BANG

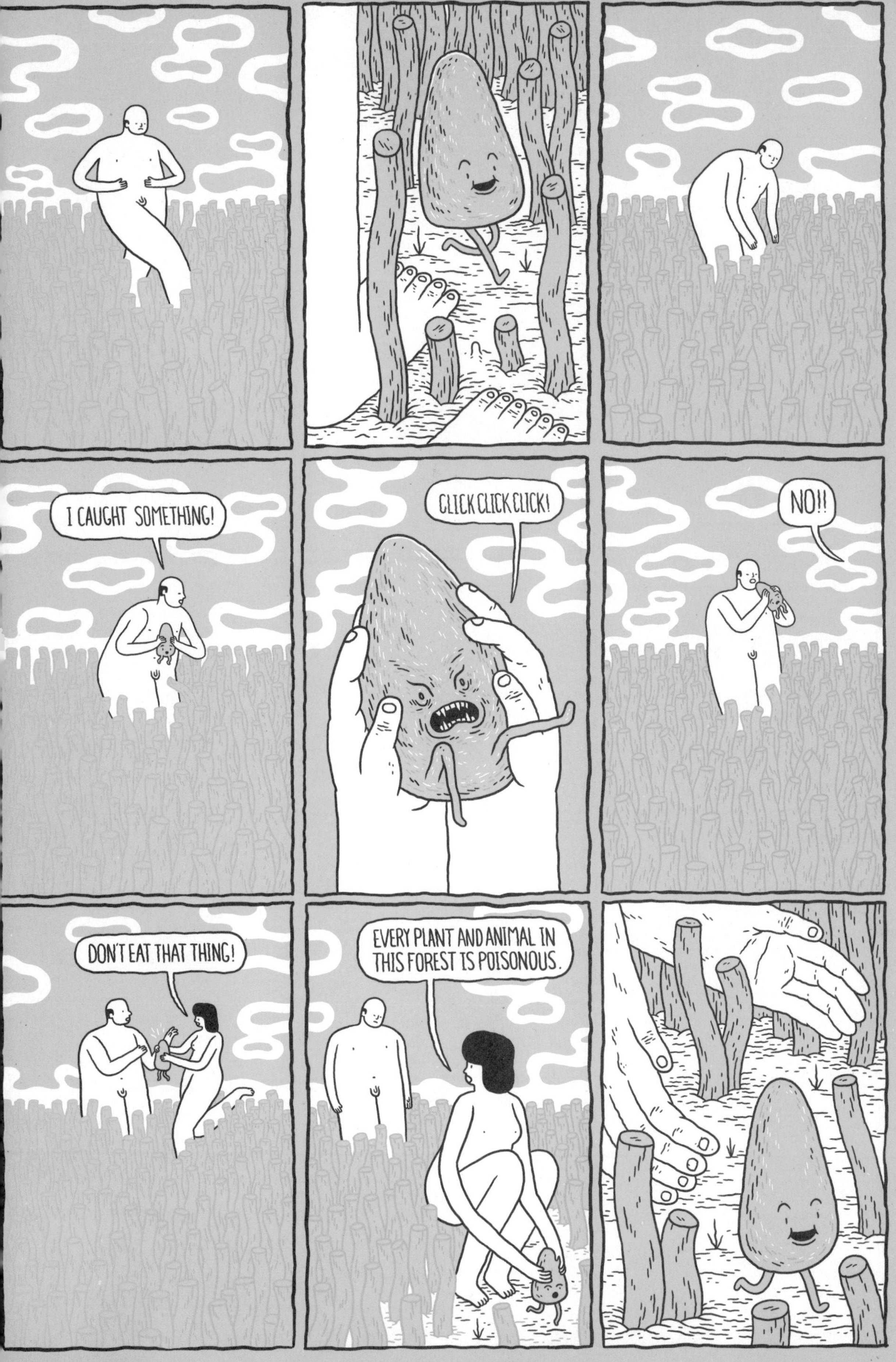
I CAUGHT SOMETHING!
CLICK CLICK CLICK!
NO!!
DON'T EAT THAT THING!
EVERY PLANT AND ANIMAL IN THIS FOREST IS POISONOUS.

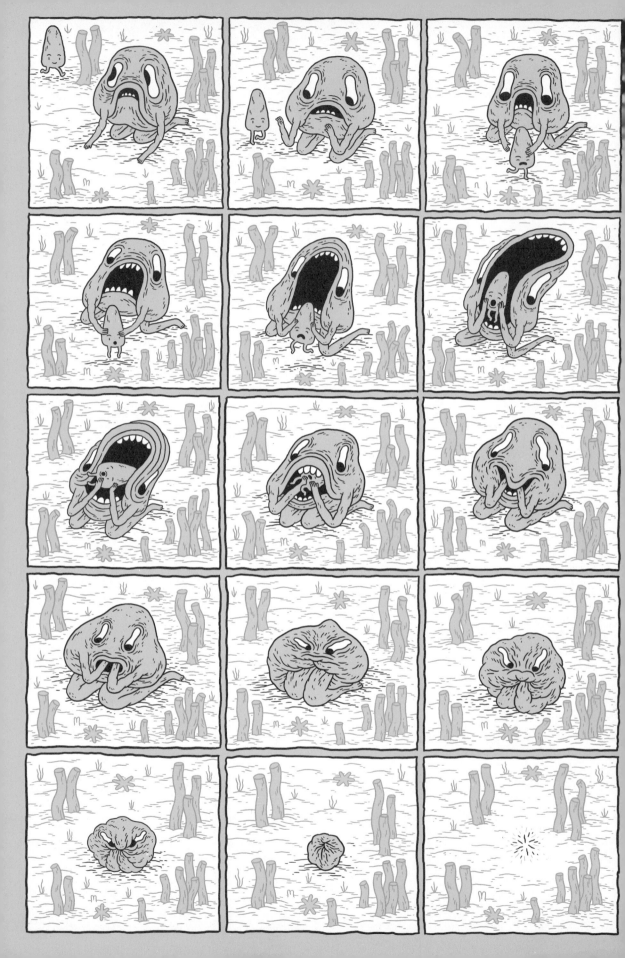

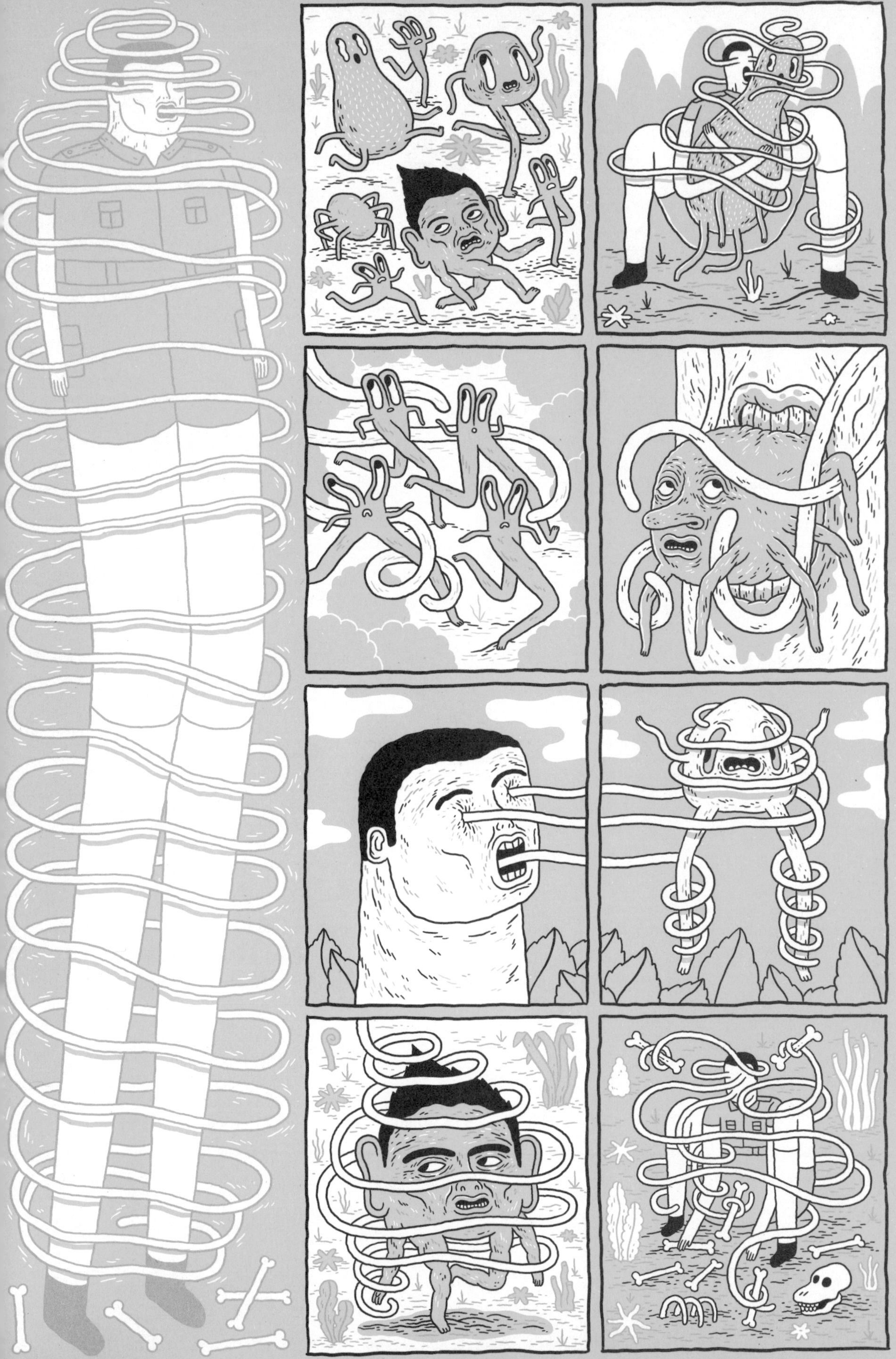

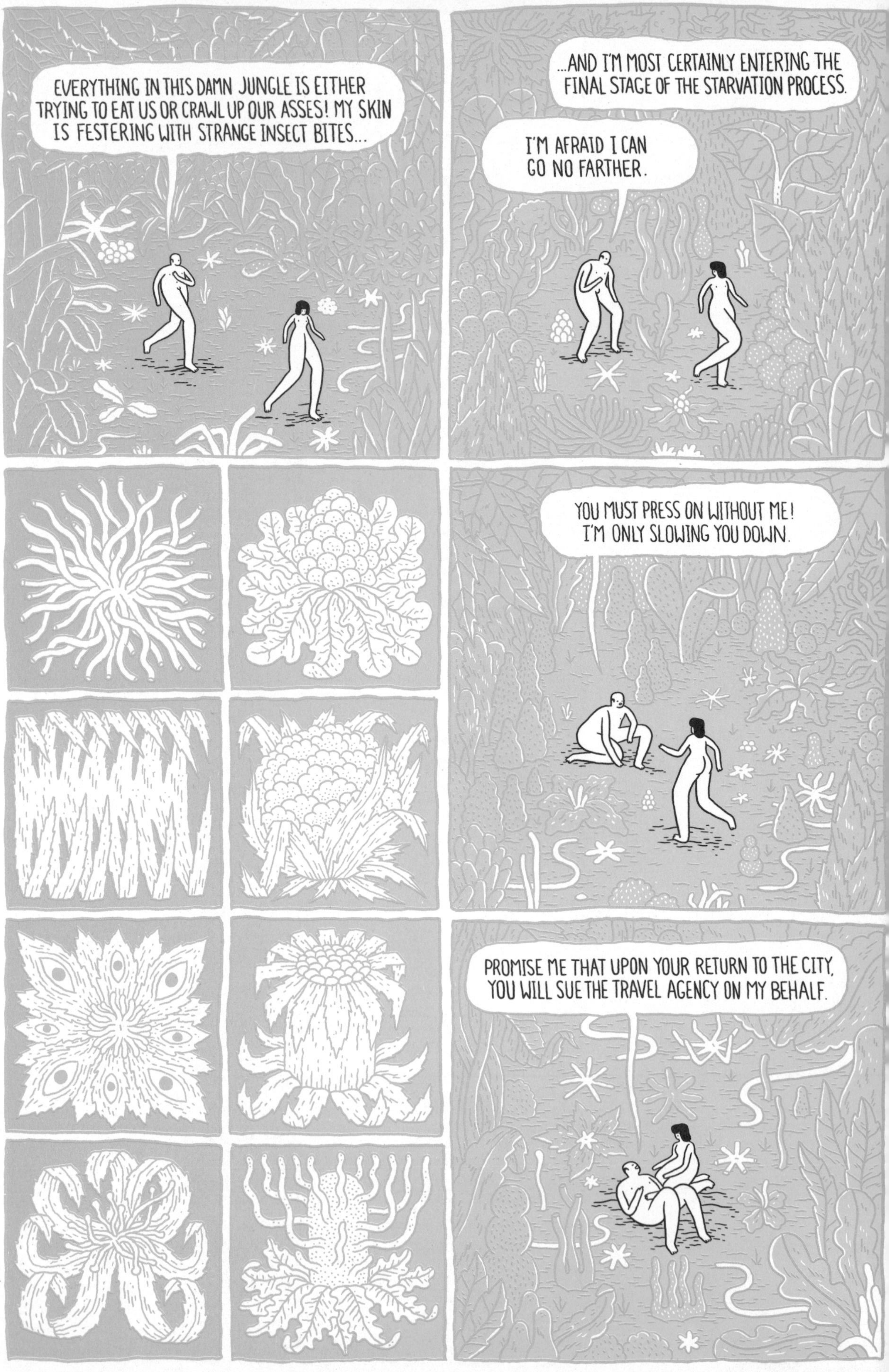
EVERYTHING IN THIS DAMN JUNGLE IS EITHER TRYING TO EAT US OR CRAWL UP OUR ASSES! MY SKIN IS FESTERING WITH STRANGE INSECT BITES...
...AND I'M MOST CERTAINLY ENTERING THE FINAL STAGE OF THE STARVATION PROCESS.
I'M AFRAID I CAN GO NO FARTHER.
YOU MUST PRESS ON WITHOUT ME! I'M ONLY SLOWING YOU DOWN.
PROMISE ME THAT UPON YOUR RETURN TO THE CITY, YOU WILL SUE THE TRAVEL AGENCY ON MY BEHALF.

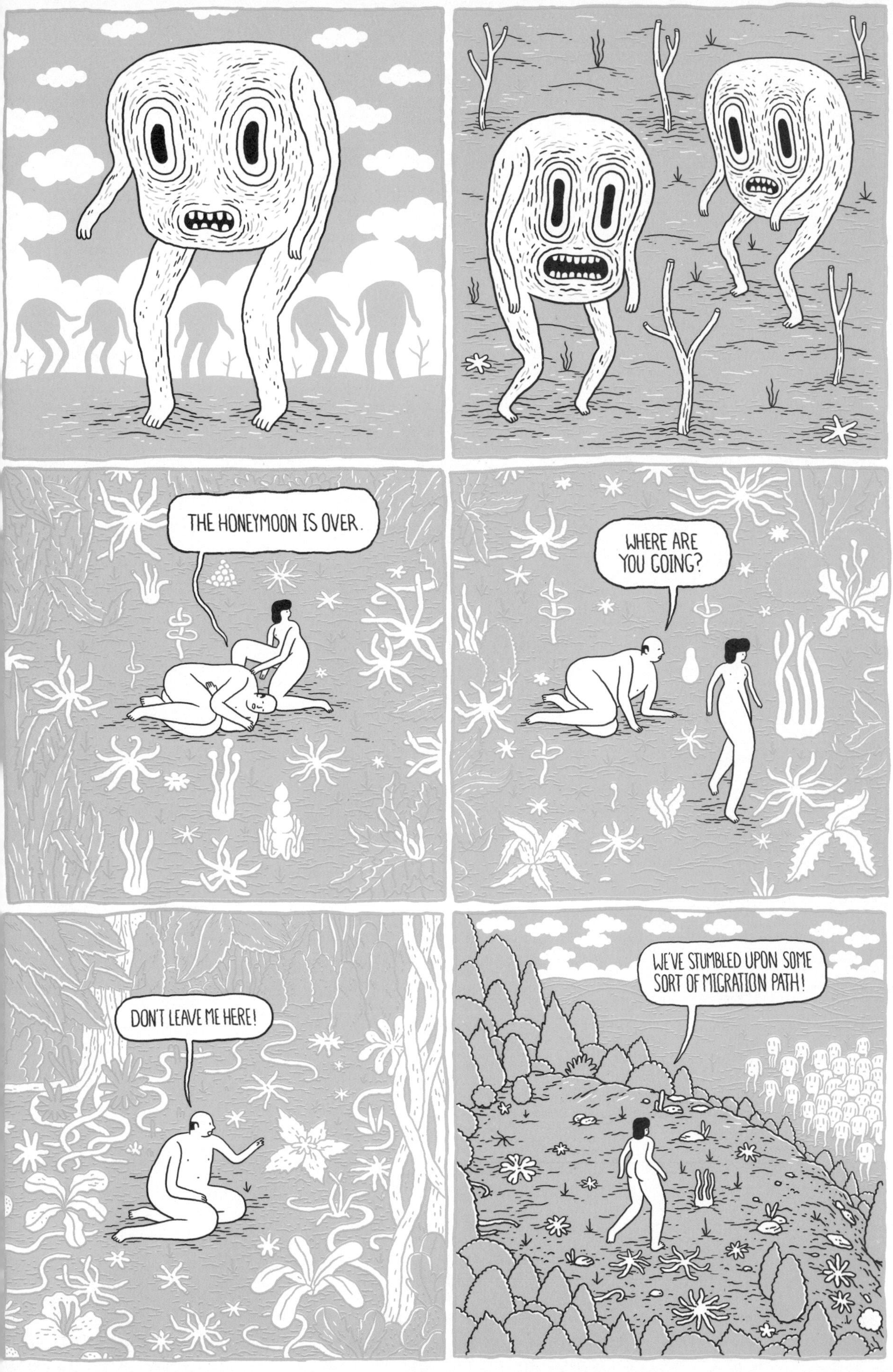
THE HONEYMOON IS OVER.
WHERE ARE YOU GOING?
DON'T LEAVE ME HERE!
WE'VE STUMBLED UPON SOME SORT OF MIGRATION PATH!

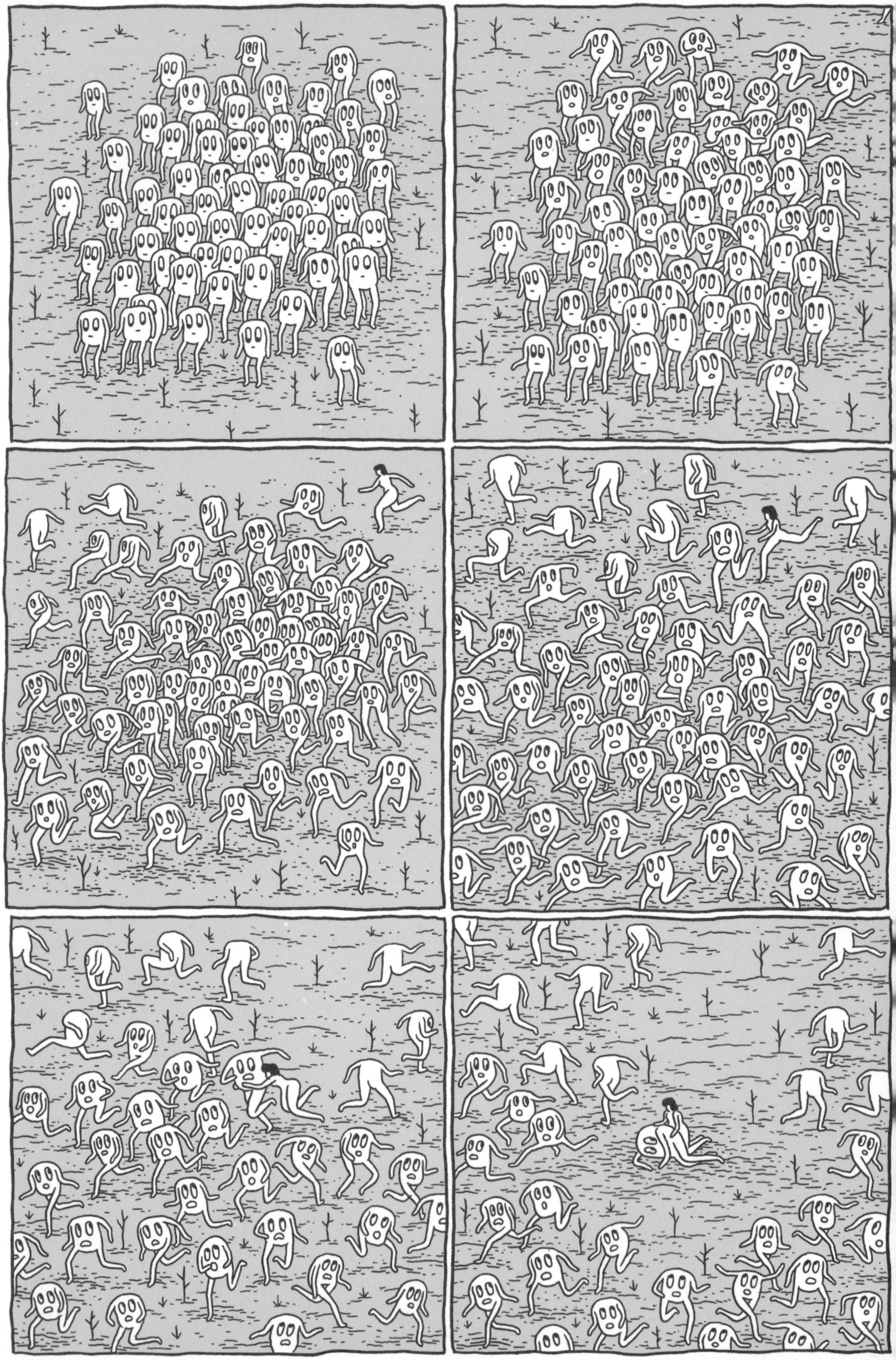

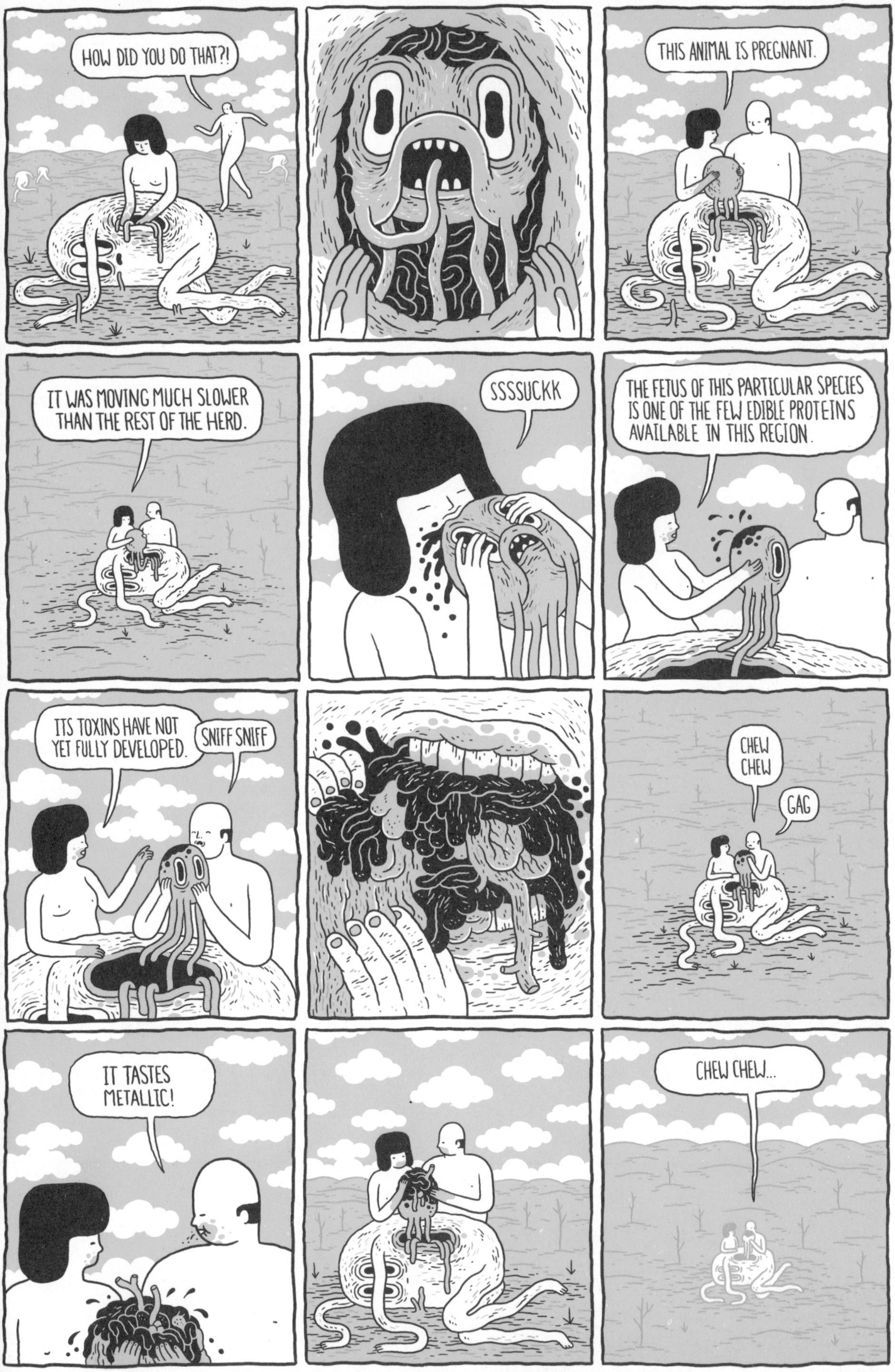
HOW DID YOU DO THAT?!
THIS ANIMAL IS PREGNANT.
IT WAS MOVING MUCH SLOWER THAN THE REST OF THE HERD.
SSSSUCKK
THE FETUS OF THIS PARTICULAR SPECIES IS ONE OF THE FEW EDIBLE PROTEINS AVAILABLE IN THIS REGION.
ITS TOXINS HAVE NOT YET FULLY DEVELOPED.
SNIFF SNIFF
CHEW CHEW
GAG
IT TASTES METALLIC!
CHEW CHEW...

PREDETERMINED PATTERNS OF THINKING ARE INADEQUATE. YOUR THOUGHTS ARE NOTHING MORE THAN MEANINGLESS CLOUDS PASSING ACROSS AN ENDLESSLY BLUE SKY.

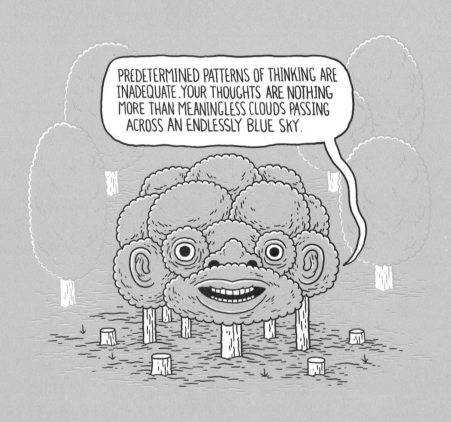

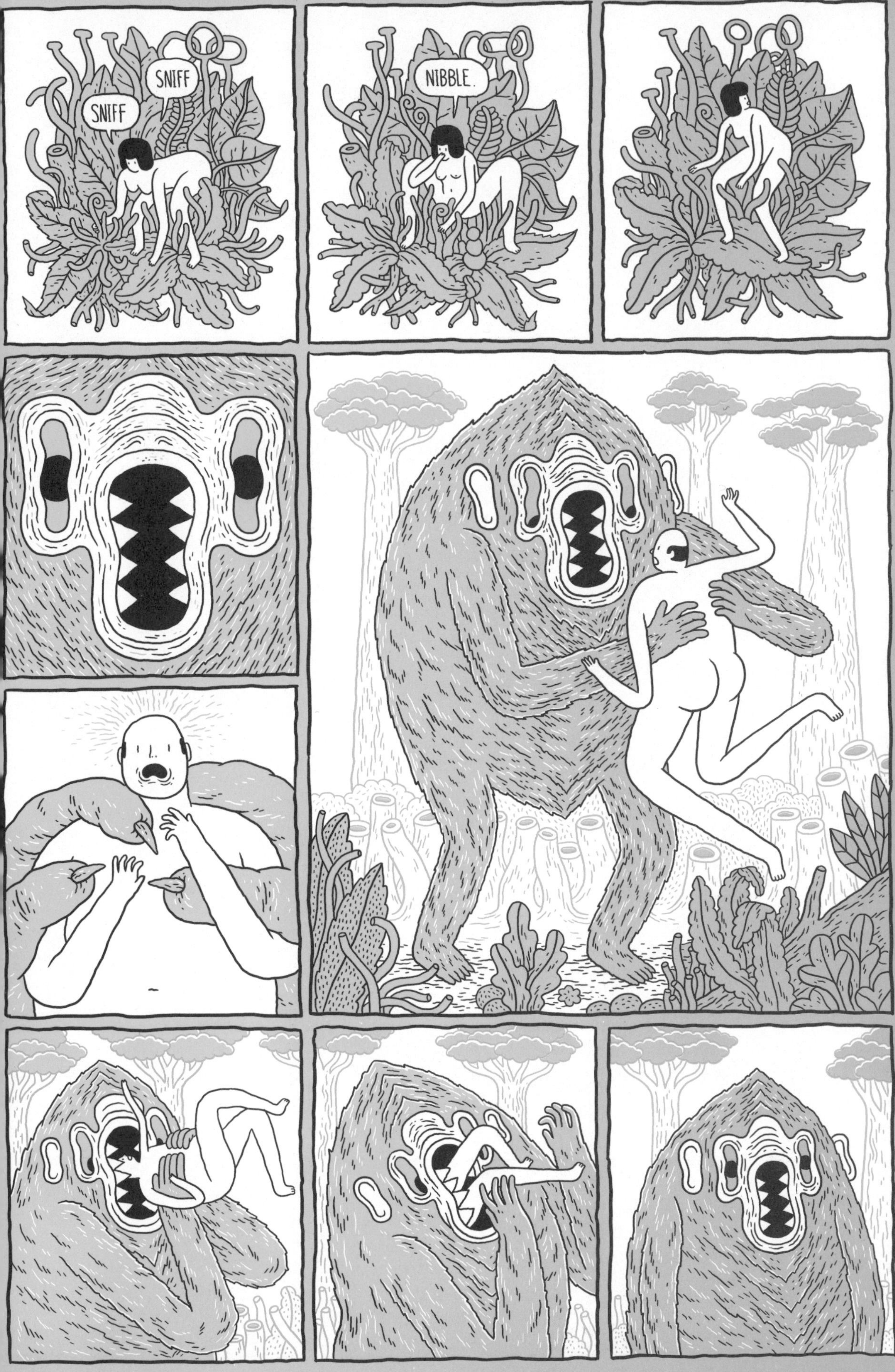
SNIFF
SNIFF
NIBBLE.

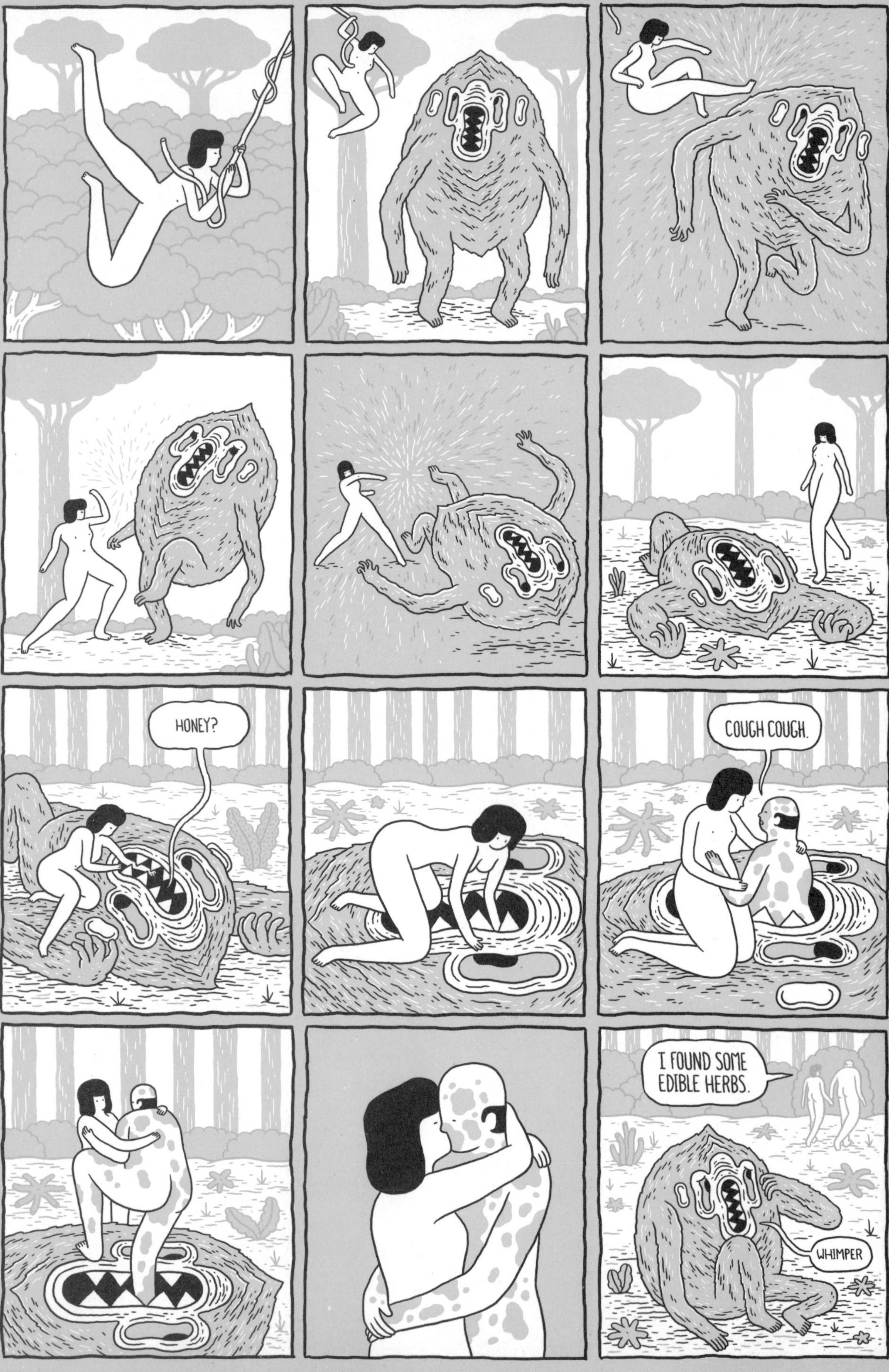
HONEY?
COUGH COUGH.
I FOUND SOME EDIBLE HERBS.
WHIMPER

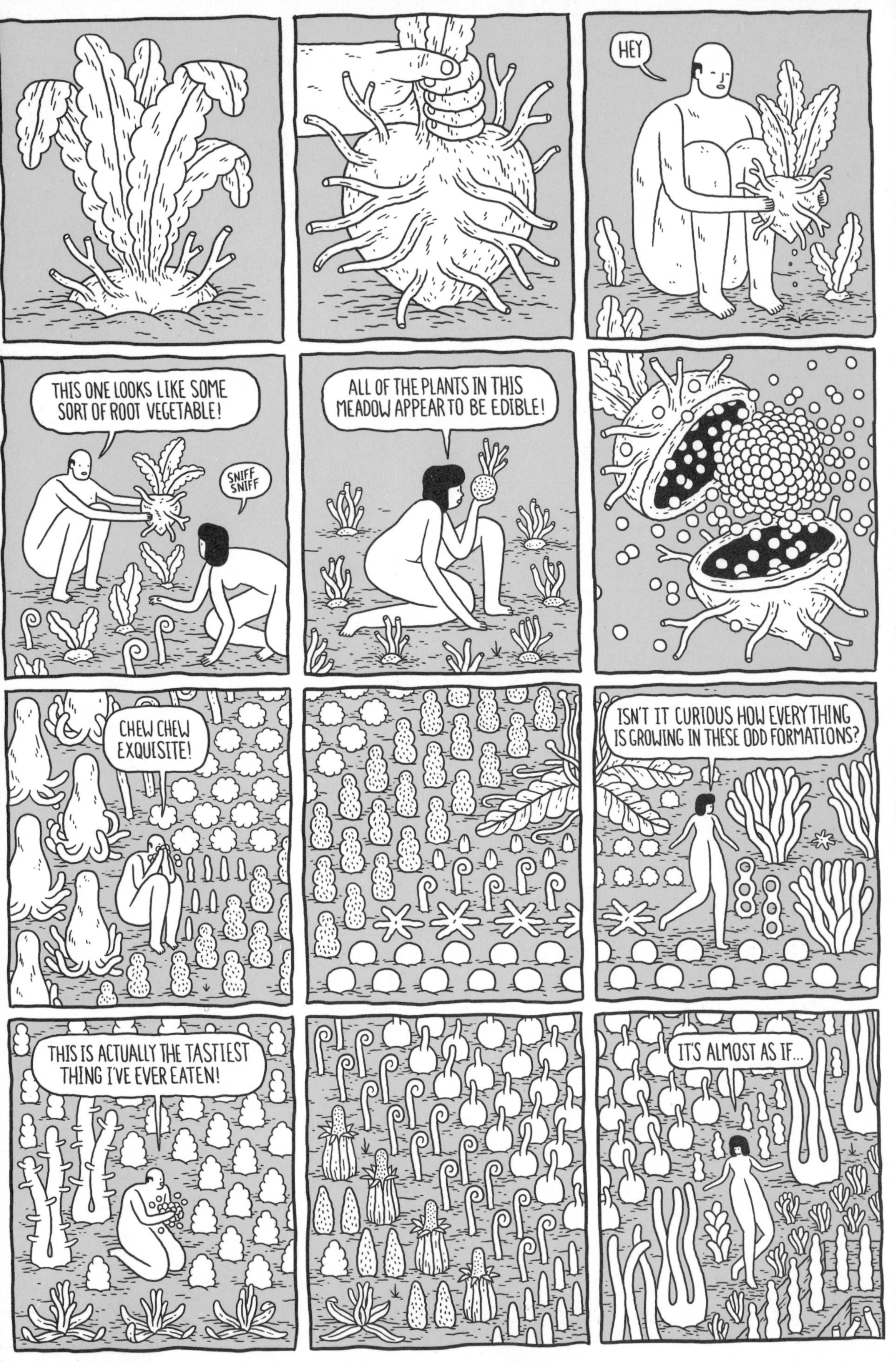
HEY
THIS ONE LOOKS LIKE SOME SORT OF ROOT VEGETABLE!
SNIFF SNIFF
ALL OF THE PLANTS IN THIS MEADOW APPEAR TO BE EDIBLE!
CHEW CHEW EXQUISITE!
ISN'T IT CURIOUS HOW EVERYTHING IS GROWING IN THESE ODD FORMATIONS?
THIS IS ACTUALLY THE TASTIEST THING I'VE EVER EATEN!
IT'S ALMOST AS IF...

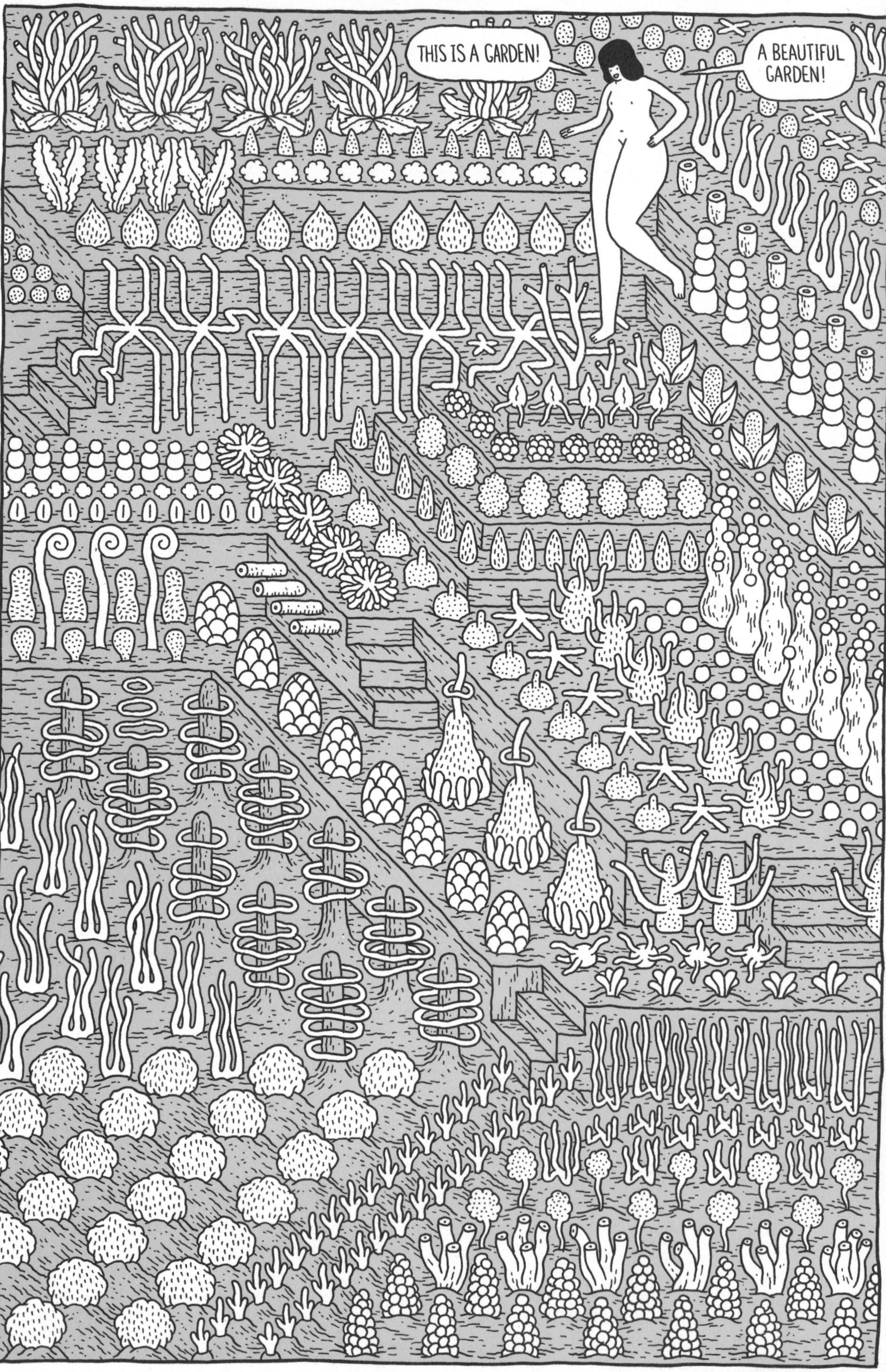
THIS IS A GARDEN!
A BEAUTIFUL GARDEN!

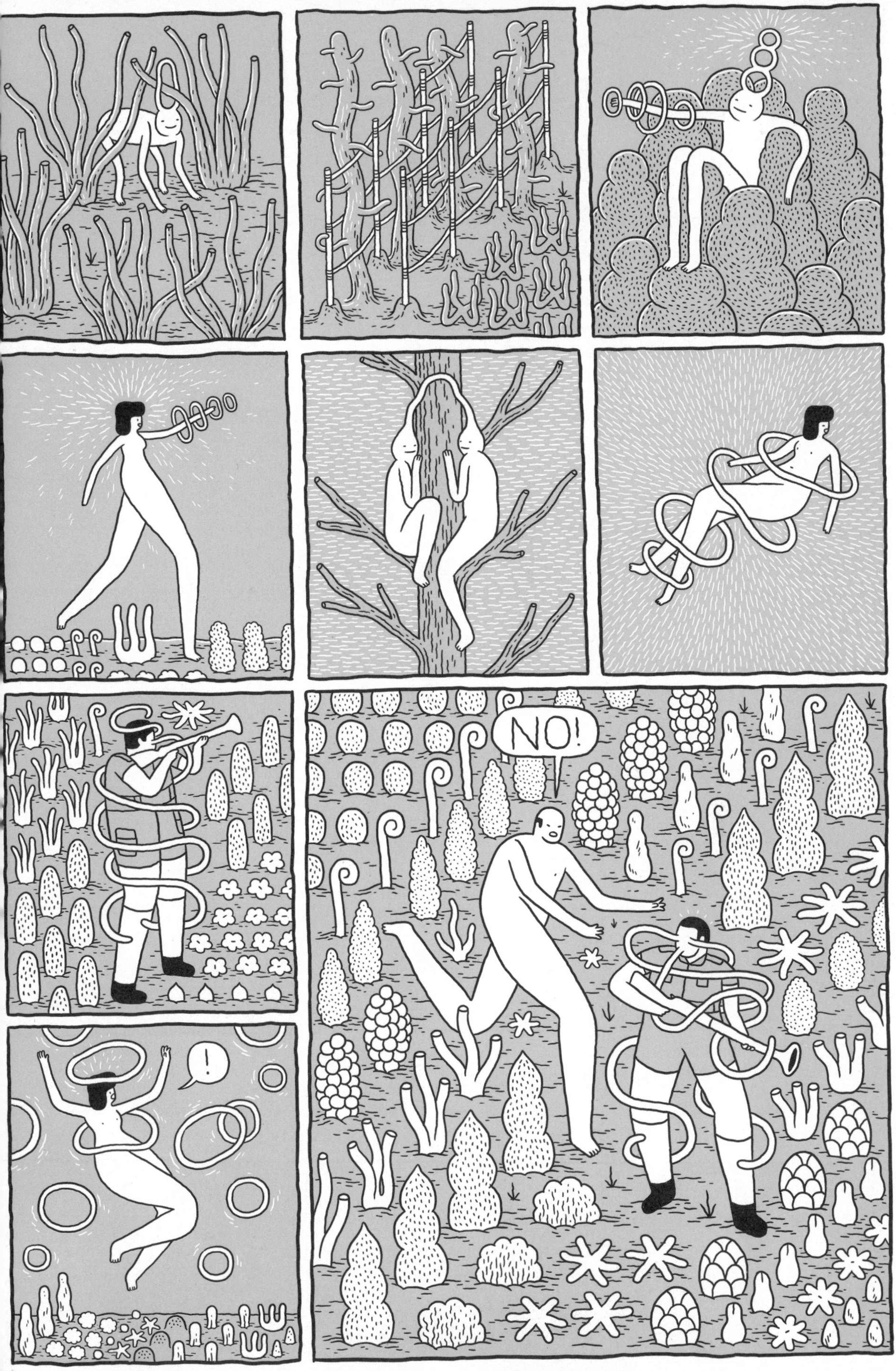
NO!
!

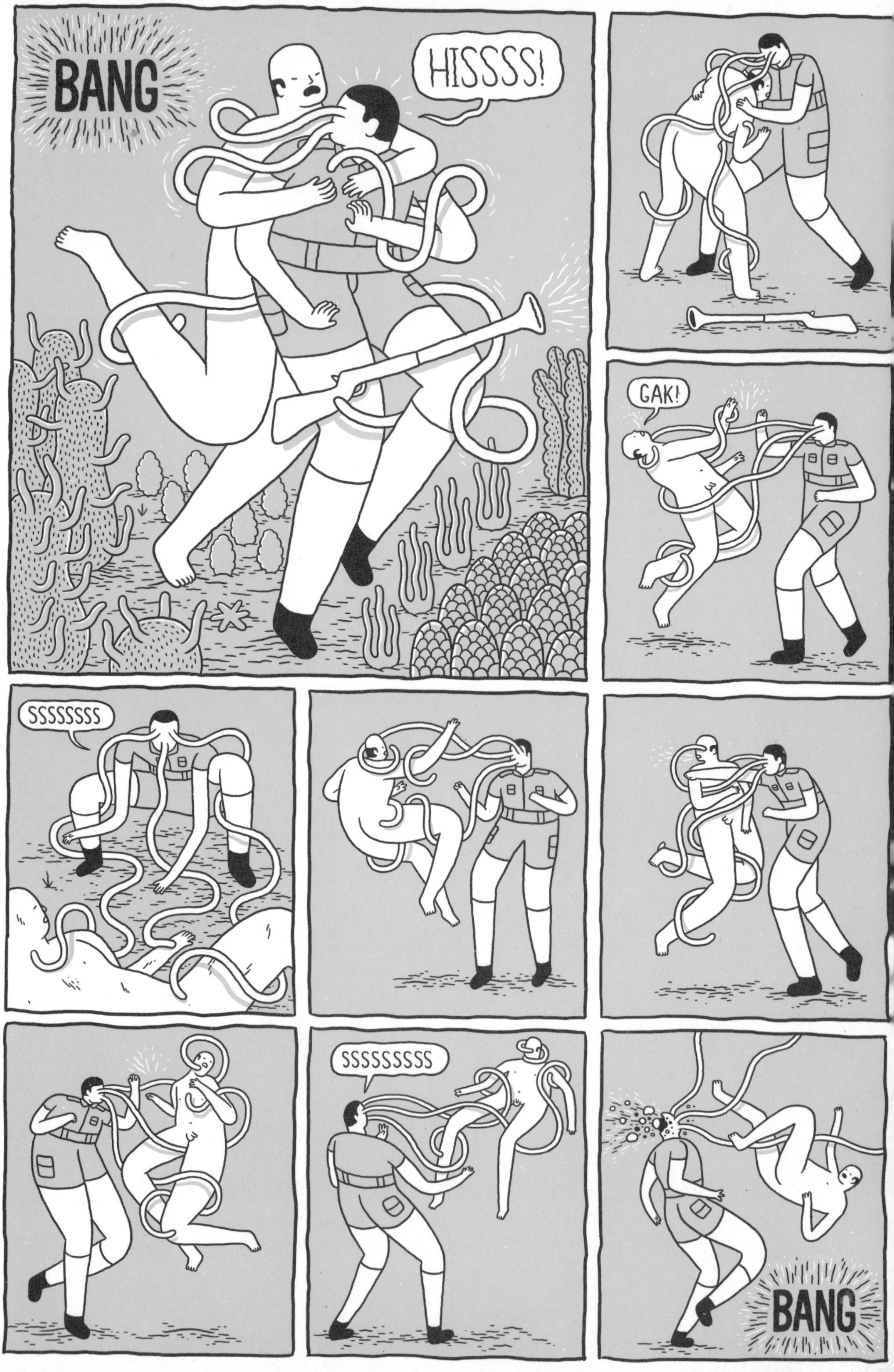
BANG
HISSSS!
GAK!
SSSSSSSS
SSSSSSSSS
BANG

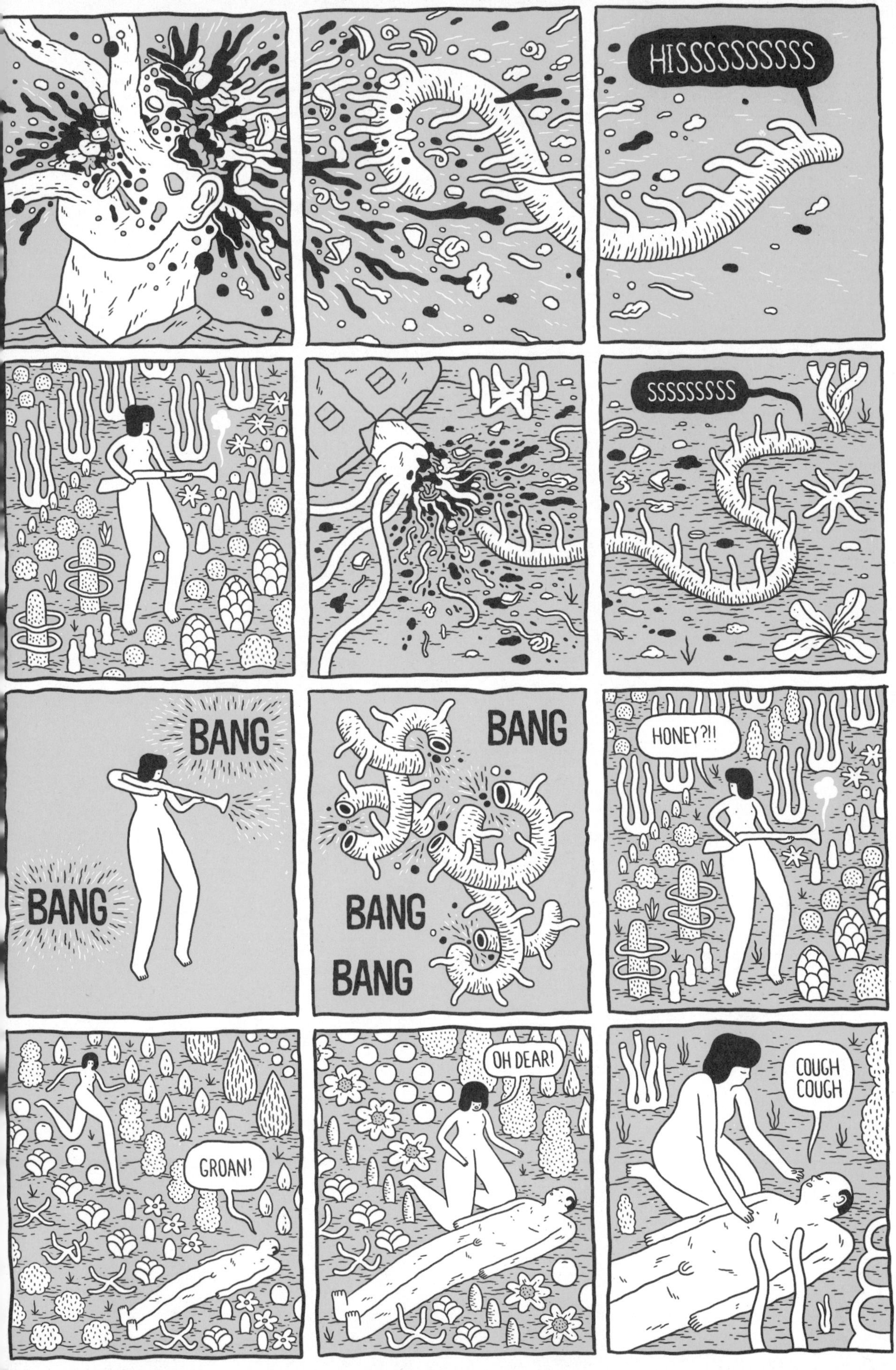
HISSSSSSSSSS
SSSSSSSSS
BANG
BANG
BANG
BANG
BANG
HONEY?!!
GROAN!
OH DEAR!
COUGH
COUGH

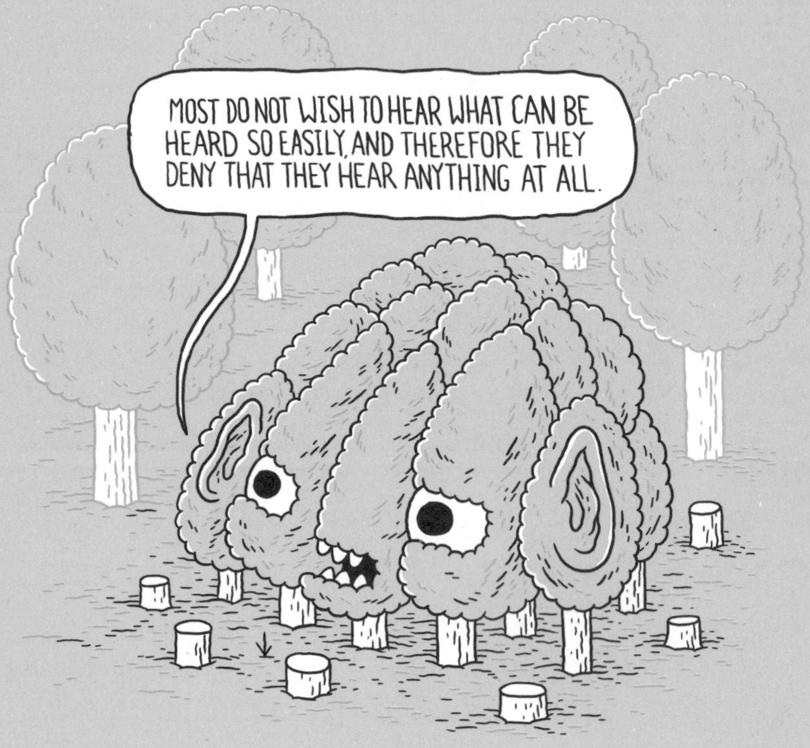
MOST DO NOT WISH TO HEAR WHAT CAN BE HEARD SO EASILY, AND THEREFORE THEY DENY THAT THEY HEAR ANYTHING AT ALL.

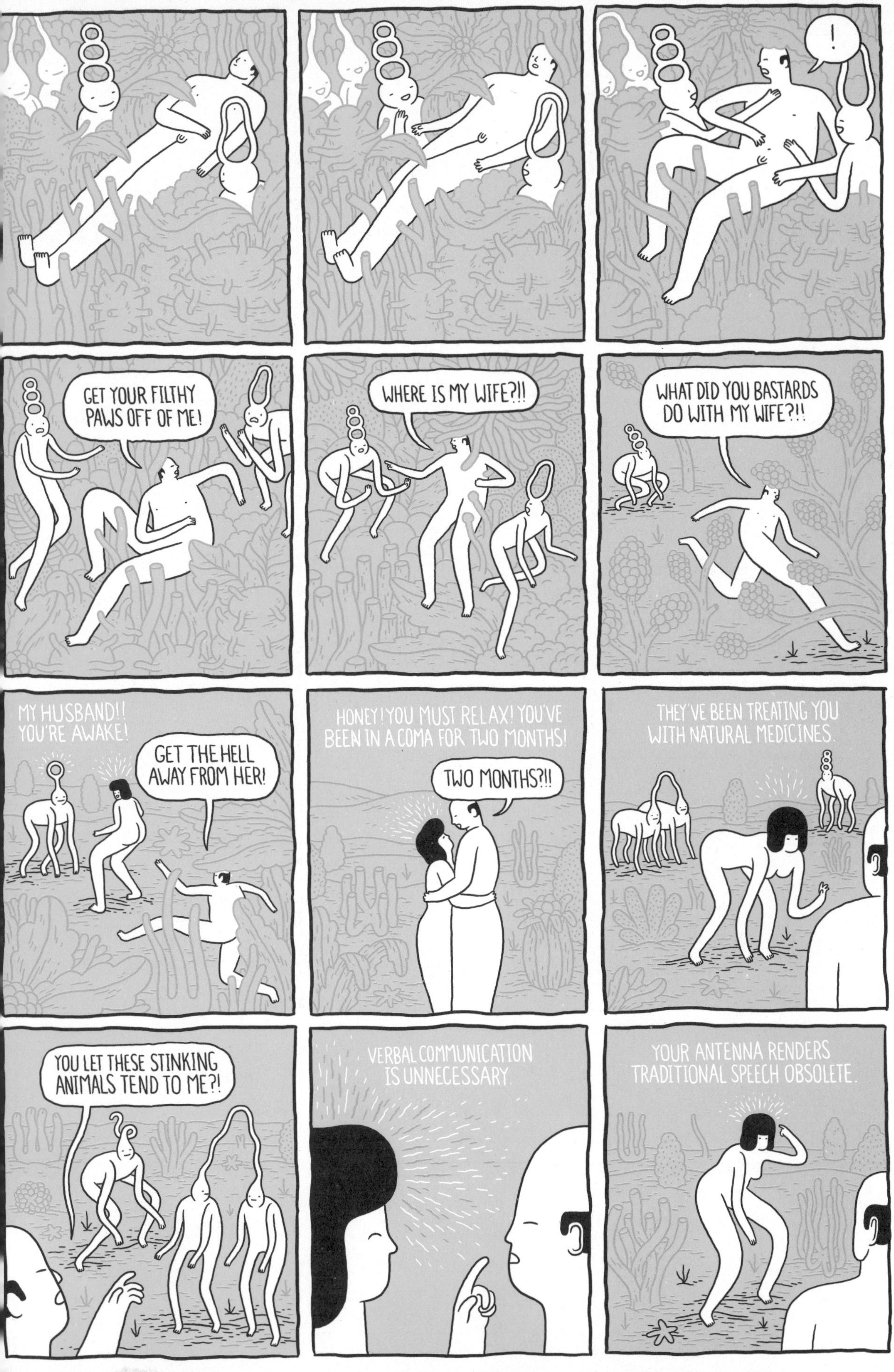
!
GET YOUR FILTHY PAWS OFF OF ME!
WHERE IS MY WIFE?!!
WHAT DID YOU BASTARDS DO WITH MY WIFE?!!
MY HUSBAND!! YOU'RE AWAKE!
GET THE HELL AWAY FROM HER!
HONEY! YOU MUST RELAX! YOU'VE BEEN IN A COMA FOR TWO MONTHS!
TWO MONTHS?!!
THEY'VE BEEN TREATING YOU WITH NATURAL MEDICINES.
YOU LET THESE STINKING ANIMALS TEND TO ME?!
VERBAL COMMUNICATION IS UNNECESSARY.
YOUR ANTENNA RENDERS TRADITIONAL SPEECH OBSOLETE.

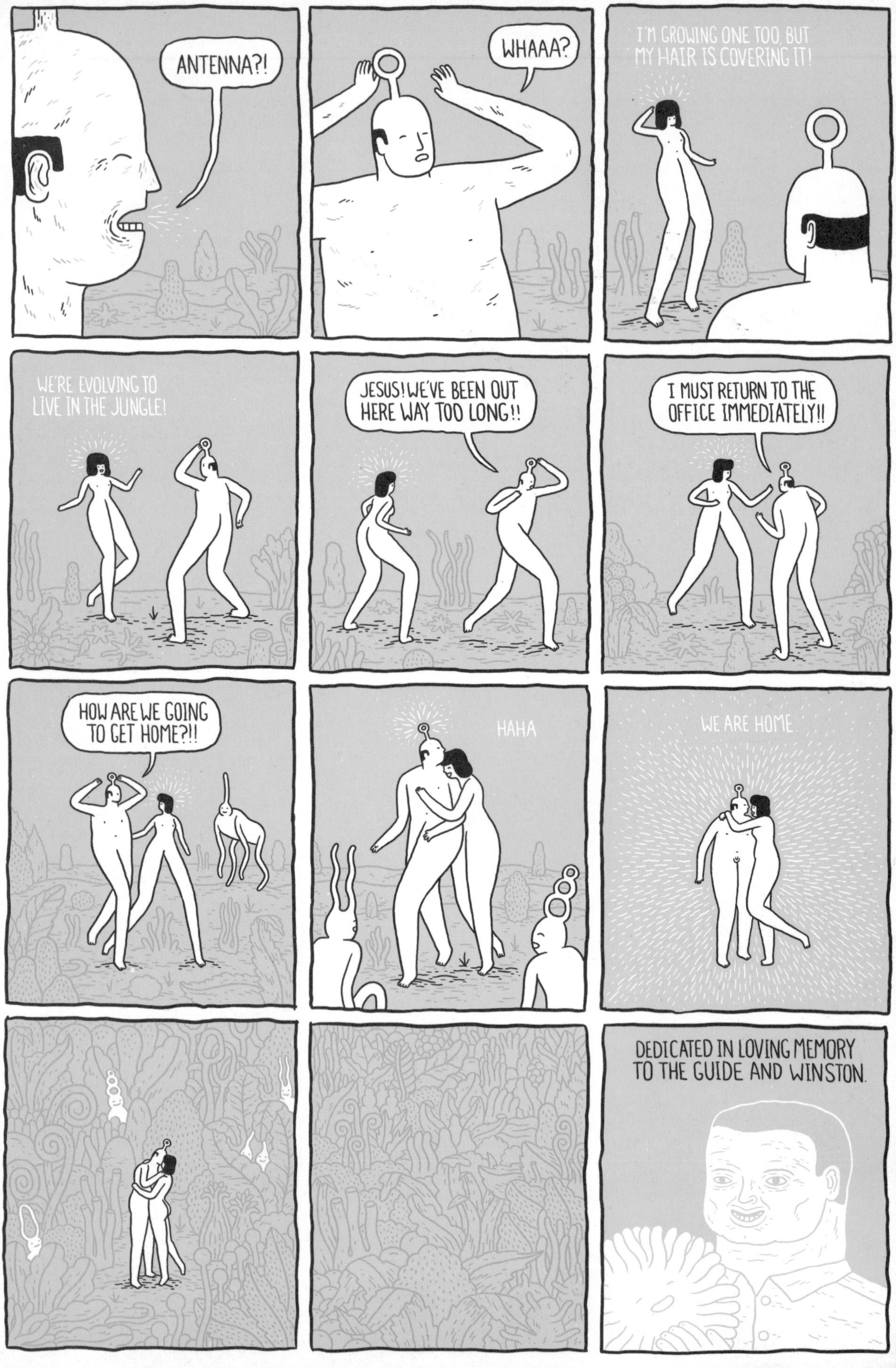
ANTENNA?!
WHAAA?
I'M GROWING ONE TOO, BUT MY HAIR IS COVERING IT!
WE'RE EVOLVING TO LIVE IN THE JUNGLE!
JESUS! WE'VE BEEN OUT HERE WAY TOO LONG!!
I MUST RETURN TO THE OFFICE IMMEDIATELY!!
HOW ARE WE GOING TO GET HOME?!!
HAHA
WE ARE HOME
DEDICATED IN LOVING MEMORY TO THE GUIDE AND WINSTON.